Reading and Writing for Today's Adults

Voyager

4

Beverly J. Smith

Advisers to the Series

Mary Dunn Siedow
Director
North Carolina Literacy Resource Center
Raleigh, NC

Linda Thistlethwaite
Associate Director
The Central Illinois Adult Education Service Center
Western Illinois University
Macomb, IL

Reviewer

LaVelle Franklin
Instructor
Project Learn to Read
San Antonio, TX

New Readers Press

Acknowledgments

Baker, Mark. Reprinted with the permission of Simon & Schuster, Inc. and International Creative Management from COPS: THEIR LIVES IN THEIR OWN WORDS by Mark Baker. Copyright © 1985 by Mark Baker.

Brisby, Stewart, "The Artist" from THE LIGHT FROM ANOTHER COUNTRY: POETRY FROM AMERICAN PRISONS, edited by Joseph Bruchac, advisory editors: Michael Hogan and John Paul Minarik, published by Greenfield Review Press, 1984. Reprinted by permission.

Colon, Jesus. "Easy Job, Good Wages" from A PUERTO RICAN IN NEW YORK by Jesus Colon. Reprinted by permission of International Publishers.

Daniel, Charles, "Could you let me have that in traveler's checks?" Cartoon reprinted courtesy of Charlie Daniel.

Dobbins, Jim. "Barely Moving." Courtesy The National Association of Government Employees. Reprinted by permission.

Eller, Daryn. "The World's Easiest Workout," MCCALL'S Magazine, March 1995. Reprinted with permission of McCall's Magazine. Copyright 1995 by Gruner & Jahr USA Publishing.

Franks, Gary A., "The Floor Mopper." Excerpted with permission from "My First Job" compiled by Daniel R. Levine from the January 1995 Reader's Digest. Copyright © 1994 by The Reader's Digest Assn., Inc.

From "Five 'Little' People Who Changed U.S. History," in SCHOLASTIC UPDATE, January 26, 1990 issue. Copyright © 1990 by Scholastic. Reprinted by permission.

Hadfield, Linda C. From "How to Avoid Food that Makes You Sick," CURRENT HEALTH 2, Vol. 21, No. 7, March 1995. Reprint permission granted by Weekly Reader Corporation. Copyright © 1995 by Weekly Reader Corporation. All Rights Reserved.

Kearse, Victoria. From "Make Sure What You're Looking at Is Really What You See." Reprinted from COURAGE, a publication of The Learning Place, Syracuse, New York. Used with permission from the author.

Koterba, Jeff, "Americans Held Hostage" cartoon originally titled "The Other American Hostages." Reprinted with permission.

Voyager™: Voyager 4 Reading and Writing for Today's Adults
1-56420-154-6

Copyright © 1999 New Readers Press
New Readers Press
Division of ProLiteracy Worldwide
1320 Jamesville Avenue, Syracuse, New York 13210
www.newreaderspress.com

Printed in the United States of America
9 8 7 6 5 4

All proceeds from the sale of New Readers Press materials support literacy programs in the United States and worldwide.

Director of Acquistions and Development: Christina Jagger
Content Editor: Mary Hutchison
Developer: Learning Unlimited, Oak Park, IL
Developmental Editor: Karen Herzoff
Contributing Writer: Betsy Rubin
Cover Design: Gerald Russell
Photography: David Revette Photography, Inc.
Illustrator: Cheri Bladholm
Copy Editor: Jeanna H. Walsh
Designer: Kimbrly Koennecke
Artist/Illustrator: Linda Alden

Contents

Introduction

Welcome to New Readers Press's *Voyager 4.* In this book, you will build your reading, writing, listening, and speaking skills. You will improve your understanding of what you read. You will work with familiar types of reading selections, such as stories, articles, poems, and letters. You will also work with everyday forms, documents, and graphics.

This book has four units. Each unit in this book is based on a theme that reflects our day-to-day lives. In *Voyager 4,* you will be exploring these themes:

▶ Staying Healthy
▶ Get That Job!
▶ A Sense of Community
▶ Crime and the Law

Within each theme-based unit, you will find three lessons. Each lesson has the following features:

▶ **Before You Read:** a strategy to help you understand what you read
▶ **Reading:** a story, pamphlet, brochure, article, or letter written by adults, for adults
▶ **After You Read:** questions and activities about the reading
▶ **Think About It:** a reading skill that will help you understand what you read
▶ **Write About It:** an activity to improve your writing skills
▶ **Life Skill:** an activity to help you understand and interpret real-life reading material

We hope you enjoy exploring the themes and mastering the skills found in *Voyager 4.* We also invite you to continue your studies with the next book in our series, *Voyager 5.*

Student Self-Assessment #1

Before you begin the Skills Preview, do this self-assessment.
Share your responses with your instructor.

Reading	Good at this	Need help	Don't know how to do this
I can read and understand			
1. stories and poems		✓	
2. articles in magazines, newspapers, and books		✓	
3. pamphlets and brochures			
4. charts and graphs			
5. maps		✓	
6. political cartoons			
When I read, I can			
1. figure out new words by using context clues and by breaking long words into smaller parts			
2. use what I already know to help me understand			
3. try to predict what is coming next			
4. visualize what I read			
5. find key facts			
6. identify cause and effect relationships			
7. identify problems and solutions in reading selections			
8. follow a set of written directions			
9. apply information I've read to new situations			

Writing	Good at this	Need help	Don't know how to do this
I can fill out or write			
1. charts			
2. forms and applications		✓	
3. announcements			
4. songs and poems			
5. journal entries			
6. paragraphs with a topic sentence and supporting details			
7. letters to the editor			
8. directions		✓	
When I write, I can			
1. think of good ideas			
2. organize my ideas			
3. use facts, examples, or reasons to support my main ideas			
4. express myself clearly so others understand			
5. revise my writing to improve it			
6. edit my writing to correct spelling, capitalization, punctuation, and usage errors			
7. recognize fragments and run-on sentences and fix them			

Skills Preview

This preview will give you an idea of the kinds of readings and skills covered in this book. Before you begin Unit 1, please complete the entire preview. Then share your work with your instructor.

Reading Skills

Read each passage and answer the questions that follow.

Eating Right for a Healthy Heart

Heart disease is the number one killer of adults in the U.S. Yet many heart disease deaths can be prevented. One way to reduce the risk of heart disease is to eat right.

Part of eating right is limiting foods that are high in fat and cholesterol. These substances can increase the risk of heart disease. Doctors suggest we eat low amounts of the following foods:

- whole-milk products (such as whole milk and cheese)
- fatty meats (such as hot dogs, bacon, and sausage)
- fats and oils (such as margarine, lard, and butter)

- fried foods (such as fried chicken and french fries)
- many snacks and sweets (such as chips, nuts, candy bars, cakes, and cookies)

Foods that are high in starch and fiber are a much better choice, doctors say. They suggest we eat more grains, vegetables, and fruits. These foods are low in both fat and cholesterol.

On its own, a healthy diet cannot prevent heart disease. You must have a healthy lifestyle, too. Keep fit. Quit smoking. Eat right. Exercise. Your heart will thank you.

Choose the best answer to each question.

1. What is the main idea of this article?
   (1) Healthy eating reduces the risk of heart disease.
   (2) Fried foods are high in fat.
   (3) Eat foods with fiber.
   (4) Doctors recommend grains and fruit.

2. What can you do to have a healthier heart?
   (1) Drink whole milk.
   (2) Eat foods low in fat and cholesterol.
   (3) Eat foods such as chips and cakes.
   (4) Avoid foods such as grains and fruits.

A Neighborhood Park Rises from Rubble

For years I lived near a vacant lot that we in the neighborhood called the Jungle. Because it was pretty much abandoned, a teenage gang moved in and took it over. Broken bottles and garbage littered the ground. The gang scrawled graffiti on what was left of the fence. They even dragged in old car seats to make a kind of meeting room. They scared everyone. When the gang was there, we avoided walking by the Jungle. The Jungle made our whole neighborhood seem unpleasant and dangerous.

After a while, some of the old-timers moved away. At one point, I planned to move. Then I decided it was my neighborhood, too. My neighbors agreed. We knew that if we controlled the public areas, like this vacant lot, it would be harder for the gangs to come back. A few of us decided to take back control of the vacant lot.

For the next few years, we urged the city to turn this dump into a neighborhood park. Last year we finally got our chance. The city elected a new mayor, and he formed a Community Outreach office. This office helped us form a neighborhood association.

The next step was to apply for funds. After a lot of work, our association got $125,000 in city, state, and federal funds. We used part of this money to hire a park planning company to prepare a detailed plan. The rest of the funds would be needed after we started working, to pay for trash removal, playground equipment, landscaping, and maintenance. Then we submitted the plan to the city parks department and received approval.

After getting approval, we formed a volunteer crew. The crew removed all the trash and raked the ground smooth. Some worked on making a baseball field with fencing around three sides. Others planted bushes and trees and laid sod. One group paved a path and built a brick patio area for benches. Some teenagers helped build a children's fort. Other workers erected playground equipment and a basketball hoop. After three months of hard work, we had changed the vacant lot from the Jungle to a park. In the end, we were proud of the park. Everything we had done passed the city inspection.

Now the garbage and the broken bottles are gone. Teenage gangs no longer feel free to walk in and take over—other people are in residence these days. Kids swing in the playground and play in the fort. Neighbors sit on benches and talk with each other. Teenagers shoot baskets at one end of the park.

We've had some problems, but we try to solve them right away. For example, one night someone sprayed graffiti on the new benches. We used our maintenance funds to buy paint. By the next afternoon, we had repainted the benches.

By keeping up with the problems, we hope to keep the park from turning back into what it once was. It takes constant work, but it is worth it. The park has united our neighborhood. For many, it is a dream come true.

Choose the best answer to each question.

3. What was the major problem with the Jungle?
   (1) litter on the ground
   (2) abandoned car seats
   (3) a gang that took over
   (4) graffiti on the fence

4. What effect did the gang have on the neighborhood?
   (1) People were afraid to walk outside.
   (2) Police patrolled almost constantly.
   (3) Gang wars took place.
   (4) Neighbors ignored the gang.

5. To solve the problem with the Jungle, neighbors
   (1) moved away
   (2) called the police
   (3) turned it into a park
   (4) painted the benches

6. In order to build a park, what did the neighborhood association do first?
   (1) repainted the park benches
   (2) applied for funds
   (3) built a fort for children
   (4) removed the trash

Who's Hiring?

The health services field is one of the hottest employers in the U.S. Between 1992 and 2005, this field is projected to hire up to 4.2 million people in newly created jobs. Why the big need for health-care workers? One reason is improved medical knowledge. Doctors can now treat many diseases they could not treat years ago. Thus, they can treat more patients. Another reason is the aging U.S. population. More people are living longer. As they age, they will need more medical care than they have needed in the past.

There are many different jobs in the health services field. There are many different job sites, too. Look at the graph below. It shows the projected number of new jobs at different health services sites.

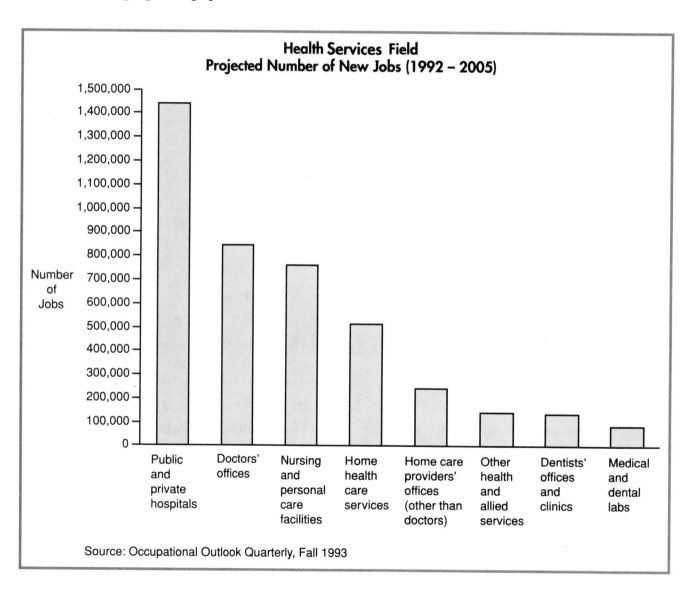

Health Services Field
Projected Number of New Jobs (1992 – 2005)

Number of Jobs

Categories: Public and private hospitals; Doctors' offices; Nursing and personal care facilities; Home health care services; Home care providers' offices (other than doctors); Other health and allied services; Dentists' offices and clinics; Medical and dental labs

Source: Occupational Outlook Quarterly, Fall 1993

Choose the best answer to each question.

7. What is the main idea of this article?
   (1) Doctors have better medical knowledge today than in the past.
   (2) The U.S. population is aging.
   (3) There are many new jobs in the health services field.
   (4) Hospitals will have more than 1 million new jobs by 2005.

8. The health field will create new jobs for
   (1) mainly doctors
   (2) few home health care workers
   (3) more lab workers than hospital workers
   (4) up to 4.2 million people by 2005

9. The greatest number of new jobs will be in
   (1) hospital settings
   (2) dental clinics and offices
   (3) private homes
   (4) doctors' offices

10. One reason for the growth in the health services field is
   (1) more people stay young longer
   (2) there are more diseases
   (3) medical knowledge has improved
   (4) more people are living together

Write About It

On a separate piece of paper, write about the topic below. Use the checklist below to revise your draft. Then give your draft to your instructor for feedback.

Topic Our jails are overflowing. Many people believe that first-time offenders who commit nonviolent crimes should not be sent to jail. They should be ordered to do community service instead. Do you agree? Why or why not? Write one or more paragraphs to explain your opinion.

Revising Checklist

Revise your draft. Check that your draft

_____ clearly states your opinion

_____ gives reasons to support your opinion

_____ explains your reasons

Skills Preview Answers

Reading Skills

1. (1)		**6.** (2)	
2. (2)		**7.** (3)	
3. (3)		**8.** (4)	
4. (1)		**9.** (1)	
5. (3)		**10.** (3)	

Write About It

Make changes on your first draft to improve your writing. Then recopy your draft and share it with your instructor.

Skills Chart

The questions in the Skills Preview assess familiarity with the following skills:

Question	Skill
1	main idea
2	apply information
3	problems and solutions
4	cause and effect
5	problems and solutions
6	sequence of events
7	main idea
8	key facts
9	key facts
10	cause and effect

Unit 1 Staying Healthy

We get a lot of advice on how to stay healthy. Every week there are newspaper articles and radio and TV programs with new ideas for better health. Sometimes it is hard to know what to believe. But there are some tried and true ways to work toward better health. You will read about some of these in Unit 1. Before you read, think about your own health. Are you in good health? Do you have to work at staying healthy?

▶ **Be an Active Reader**

As you read the selections in this unit
- Put a question mark (?) by things you do not understand.
- <u>Underline</u> words you do not know. Try to use context clues to figure them out.

After you read each selection in this unit
- Reread sections you marked with a question mark (?). If they still do not make sense, discuss them with a partner or your instructor.
- Look at words you <u>underlined</u>. Discuss any words you still don't understand with a partner or your instructor, or look them up in a dictionary.

Lesson 1

LEARNING GOALS

Strategy: Use your prior experience
Reading: Read a story
Skill: Recognize problems and solutions
Writing: Write a paragraph about Pat
Life Skill: Read medicine labels

Before You Read

In the story "I've Got to Change," Pat needs to follow some health tips. Think about your own **prior experience,** things that you have done in the past. Put a check before each health tip that you have followed in the past.

_____ Eat fruits and vegetables for snacks.

_____ Compare food labels to check fat content.

_____ Drink natural fruit juices.

_____ Don't eat a lot of candy.

_____ Walk instead of ride whenever possible.

_____ Exercise three times a week for at least 20 minutes each time.

Preview the Reading

Before you read "I've Got to Change," preview it. Look at the pictures. Think about changes you have made in your own life to improve your health. What changes do you think Pat will consider?

► **Use the Strategy**

In this story, Pat is not taking good care of herself. When she learns that her daughter is worried about her, she decides to make a change. In your experience, what can cause people to stop taking care of themselves? What effect can loved ones have when this happens?

I've Got to Change

It was early in March. Pat opened her front door and sighed. Another work day was over. As usual, she settled down to watch a TV program. There was a box of chocolates nearby. As Pat was picking out a chocolate, she overheard Rachel, her 10-year-old daughter, talking about her. She turned down the TV to listen.

Rachel was in the next room talking with her best friend. "I bet my mom won't go on our class hike this year. I wish she would. Before Dad died she used to help out a lot at school. She doesn't even walk our dog Taffy anymore. Now she gets so tired. She wouldn't be able to keep up."

Pat got out of her chair and tiptoed closer to the door.

"I love my mom, but she's really in bad shape. I just don't think she takes care of herself anymore. I wish she did."

Pat walked back to her chair and sank into it. She was surprised and worried. She hadn't realized how her daughter felt about her. Rachel was everything to her.

Pat got up and started pacing the floor. She glanced in the hall mirror. Then she stopped. She looked long and hard at herself. She could hardly believe what she saw—an overweight, tired-looking woman. She still had a piece of chocolate in her hand.

Pat needed to talk with someone about her situation. She wanted help. But she didn't want to call her sister or her friend Kari. She didn't need criticism—not today. Finally, she decided to call the health clinic she took Rachel to. Maybe someone there could give her advice. It was quarter to five, just enough time to phone. Pat threw the piece of candy away, rushed upstairs, and dialed the phone.

◀ Check-in

Why has Pat stopped taking care of herself? In your experience, is this a common reason? What effect did Rachel's comments have on Pat?

A receptionist answered, "Mason Health Clinic. How can I help you?"

Pat responded, "Aah, well . . . I need to talk with a doctor."

"Is this an emergency?" asked the receptionist.

"Yes—I mean—no. But I need to see someone soon," replied Pat. "It's about my general health. I'm overweight and run-down."

"A nurse practitioner can see you tomorrow afternoon at 4:30," the receptionist said. "Do you want this appointment?"

Pat hesitated. She liked to go right home after work and collapse in front of the TV. Then Rachel's comments came back to her. Pat responded, "Yes, I do want that appointment. I'll be there tomorrow at 4:30."

The next day at the health clinic, Pat described her worries to Kathy, the nurse practitioner. Pat said, "I feel awful. What my daughter said has upset me very much. I need some advice."

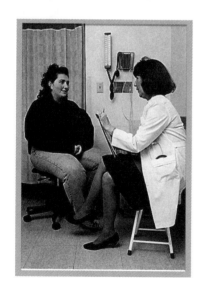

Kathy listened without interrupting. She thought about her own experience as a mother. She knew that sometimes it hurts to hear what your kids have to say. She also knew that what her kids told her was often very important.

When Pat was finished, Kathy explained to her that she could work on her weight and energy level. "Pat, there are no miracle cures. But little by little you can bring down your weight and increase your energy."

Pat was surprised to learn how her weight affected her health. Extra weight could affect her blood pressure and the condition of her heart. Pat had put on 30 pounds since her husband's death last year. Her blood pressure had gone up also.

Kathy told Pat she could begin to change that day. "You need to exercise instead of watching TV. You can take the dog for a walk every day. Walking is excellent exercise."

Then Kathy discussed diet. "For snacks, you should eat fruits and vegetables instead of candy. Cut up carrot sticks and keep them in the refrigerator. Plain popcorn is another good snack."

Kathy described healthy meals and explained the importance of eating three meals a day. "Don't skip meals. That will keep you from getting hungry for the wrong foods," she told Pat.

Kathy also spoke to Pat about high blood pressure. "You may need to take medicine if diet and exercise don't bring down your blood pressure." Kathy asked Pat to come back in six weeks to have her blood pressure checked again.

Check-in ▶ What do you think Pat will do now? Do you think Pat will try to follow Kathy's advice?

On her way home, Pat headed straight to the supermarket. Out of habit, she hesitated at the candy shelves, then hurried by. She filled her cart with fruit juices, fresh fruits, and vegetables, along with chicken for dinner and tuna for lunches.

When Rachel came home from soccer practice, she was amazed to see her mother in the kitchen fixing a salad. "What's up, Mom? Why aren't you watching TV?"

"You and I are going to sit down and eat a real meal together," replied her mother. Rachel was glad to hear that. She was tired of frozen dinners.

Suddenly Pat stopped and turned to her daughter. "Rachel, I'm going to take Taffy out for a walk. I'll be back in about twenty minutes. While I'm gone could you please check the chicken to be sure it doesn't burn?"

Rachel exclaimed, "Mom! Are you really going to walk Taffy? I don't believe it. You haven't walked her in ages."

"Well I'm going to now, Rachel. Could you find her leash?"

While Rachel looked for the leash, Pat slipped on her coat and stuck the box of chocolates inside her coat pocket. With Taffy on a leash, Pat stepped out of the house. She walked 10 blocks to find a Dumpster. Without stopping, Pat threw the candy into it. She felt as though she were starting a new chapter in her life.

She said to herself, "This is going to be hard. Very hard. I'll have to take one hour at a time, but I can change. And I *will* go with Rachel on her class hike in June."

She turned around with a feeling of triumph and headed home to eat a healthy meal with her daughter.

▶ **Final Check-in**

In your experience, do sudden changes like Pat's usually work? What can hinder or help her success? What effect might Rachel have on the situation?

▲▼▲

Laughter Is Good Medicine

Like Pat, many people eat because they feel low, and they think eating will make them feel better. They often choose foods that are not very good for them, however. Laughter is a nonfat way to make you feel better physically and mentally. Try it. Read the cartoon just for laughs.

After You Read

A. Comprehension Check

1. What did Pat usually do when she first came home from work? _____

_____

2. What prediction did Rachel share with her best friend? _____

_____

3. Why was Rachel worried about her mother? _____

_____

4. What caused Pat to decide to make a change? _____

_____

5. In your own words, tell the story "I've Got to Change" to a partner or to
   your instructor.

B. Revisit the Reading Strategy Use your experience to come up with ideas
to help Pat stick to her plan. On your own or with a partner, list some tips
that will help Pat get fit. Think of tips that have worked for you and for
people you know.

C. Think Beyond the Reading Think about these questions and discuss them
with a partner. Answer the questions in writing if you wish.

1. One reason Pat decided to get in shape was so that Rachel would
   not worry about her. What are some other reasons people decide to
   get in shape?
2. Do you think eating healthy foods can improve a person's mental health
   as well as physical health? In what ways?

Think About It: Recognize Problems and Solutions

We need to find solutions to problems nearly every day. To be effective, we must first identify what the problem is and what caused it. Then we must choose an appropriate way to solve the problem. This skill is called **recognizing problems and solutions.**

Many stories involve a central problem and its solution. For example, "I've Got to Change" is about Pat's problem and her attempt to solve it.

A. Look at Problems and Solutions

We can guess Pat's problem from the story's first paragraph:

▶ Pat opened her front door and sighed. Another work day was over. As usual, she settled down to watch a TV program. There was a box of chocolates nearby. As Pat was picking out a chocolate, she overheard Rachel, her 10-year-old daughter, talking about her.

Later in the story, Rachel points out what she thinks Pat's problem is:

▶ "I love my mom, but she's really in bad shape. I just don't think she takes care of herself anymore. I wish she did."

According to Rachel, what is Pat's problem and what is its cause?

mom don't tacare her self any more lack
mom did Before Dad died,

You may have said that Pat is in bad shape because she is not taking care of herself anymore. This is the central problem in the story.

Now think back to the story. How does Pat begin to solve her problem?

_____

_____

Pat calls a health clinic and makes an appointment to see a nurse practitioner. After talking with the nurse practitioner, Pat decides to adopt a healthier lifestyle. This is how she begins to solve her problem.

B. Practice You have identified Pat's problem. Now identify the solution suggested in each excerpt below.

1. ▶ Kathy told Pat she could begin to change that day. "You need to exercise instead of watching TV. You can take the dog for a walk every day. Walking is excellent exercise."

   Solution: _walk 2 o 3 times a week alist 20 Mn_

2. ▶ Then Kathy discussed diet. "For snacks, you should eat fruits and vegetables instead of candy. Cut up carrot sticks and keep them in the refrigerator. Plain popcorn is another good snack."

   Solution: _____

3. ▶ Kathy described healthy meals and explained the importance of eating three meals a day. "Don't skip meals. That will keep you from getting hungry for the wrong foods," she told Pat.

   Solution: _____

4. ▶ Kathy also spoke to Pat about high blood pressure. "You may need to take medicine if diet and exercise don't bring down your blood pressure." Kathy asked Pat to come back in six weeks to have her blood pressure checked again.

   Solution: _____

 Talk About It

People often need to change their eating habits as they grow older. Fill out this chart to compare your childhood eating habits with your current ones. Discuss it with a partner. Are your eating habits healthier now? How can you improve?

	Eating habits as a child	Eating habits as an adult
Breakfast		
Lunch		
Dinner		
Snacks		

Write About It: Write a Paragraph About Pat

Try to picture Pat's life a year after the story "I've Got to Change." In this activity, you will write a paragraph describing Pat's solutions to her problem.

A **paragraph** is a group of sentences about the same topic. Most paragraphs contain a **topic sentence**—a sentence that states the main idea of the paragraph. Paragraphs also contain **details**—information that tells about the main idea.

A. Prewriting Fill in details about the solutions you think Pat used to adopt a healthier lifestyle.

What exercise Pat tried _walk with taffy alist 20 min._

How Pat snacked _change eating_

How Pat changed her meals _eating every_

How Pat shopped _bay helthy food_

What Pat did about her blood pressure _?_

B. Writing On separate paper, write a paragraph about how Pat changed her lifestyle. Your paragraph might begin with this topic sentence: "In order to adopt a healthier lifestyle, Pat made many changes." Use the details you listed above to complete your paragraph. Add more details if you like.

▶ **Save your draft.** At the end of this unit, you will choose one of your drafts to work with further.

Life Skill: Read Medicine Labels

At times, we may need medicine. While medicine can save lives, it can be harmful if taken incorrectly. It is important to read medicine labels correctly.

Here are some words that are often found on medicine labels. Discuss these words with a partner. Write a short definition of each one.

1. indications _____

2. dosage _____

3. drug interaction precaution _____

Prescription (Rx) Medicine Guidelines

- Follow instructions on the label carefully.
- Check the dosage (how much to take) and times to take it.
- Read any warnings on the medicine label.
- Keep medicine and instructions in the original container.
- Check dates and throw away out-of-date medicine.
- Keep a record of the medicine name.
- If you don't understand something on the label, ask your doctor or pharmacist to explain it.

Practice Read the label on an empty pill bottle. Fill in the following information about the medicine.

Name of the drug _____

Dosage and time instructions _____

Quantity (QTY) _____ Discard after _____

Warnings _____

Drug interaction precautions _____

_____

Lesson 2

▶ LEARNING GOALS

Strategy: Set a purpose
Reading: Read a pamphlet
Skill: Apply information
Writing: Fill in a KWL chart
Life Skill: Read a food chart

Before You Read

Do you eat right to stay healthy? In this lesson, you will be reading a pamphlet titled "Eat More Fruits & Vegetables." Think about what you already know about the value of fruits and vegetables. Then **set a purpose** for reading by deciding what you want to learn from the article. What nutrition information about fruits and vegetables would you like to learn? Jot down some questions.

_____

_____

Preview the Reading

Preview the pamphlet by studying the title and the section headings. Look at the artwork. What kind of information do you expect to learn from this pamphlet?

Basic Food Groups	Recommended Daily Allowance
Bread, cereal, rice, and pasta	6–11 servings per day
Meat, poultry, fish, dried beans, peas, eggs, and nuts	2–3 servings per day
Milk, yogurt, and cheese	2–3 servings per day
Fruit	2–4 servings per day
Vegetables	3–5 servings per day

The food groups shown above are generally recognized as important for your health. To have a balanced diet, you should eat foods from all five groups. Which groups do you eat from most often? Which groups will the article discuss?

As you read, look for answers to the questions you wrote on page 24. What do you want to learn about a healthier diet? Use this pamphlet as a chance to learn helpful facts about healthy food.

Eat More Fruits & Vegetables

by the U.S. Department of Health and Human Services

Did you know that eating five fruits & vegetables a day is one of the most important choices you can make to help maintain your health?

Top health experts agree that increasing fruits and vegetables in the diet is essential for better health! The U.S. Department of Health and Human Services, the U.S. Department of Agriculture and the National Academy of Sciences all recommend that Americans should eat a balanced diet low in fat which includes lots of fruits and vegetables.

Fruits and vegetables may lower your risk of cancer! 35% of all cancer deaths may be related to what we eat—a diet high in fat and low in fiber.[1] Fruits and vegetables help reduce your risk of cancer. They are low in fat and are rich sources of vitamin A, vitamin C, and fiber. A low-fat diet that is low in saturated fat and cholesterol[2] and includes plenty of high fiber foods also decreases the risk of heart disease.

Eat 5 servings of fruits and vegetables a day! Top health experts recommend that you eat five servings of fruits and vegetables each day. Eat them with a variety of other foods. One serving is 1/2 cup of fruit, 3/4 cup juice, 1/2 cup cooked vegetable, 1 cup leafy vegetable, or 1/4 cup dried fruit.

Eat a variety of fruits and vegetables! All fruits and vegetables are good for you. However, be sure to include each day those that are high in vitamin A, vitamin C, and fiber. You should also have several servings of vegetables a week from the cabbage family. Vitamin supplements do not give the same health benefits as eating a variety of fruits and vegetables.

Additional health benefits. Fruits and vegetables without added fats have no cholesterol. Almost all are low in calories, fat and sodium. Some are good sources of other nutrients[3] such as folacin, potassium, and calcium. Fruits and vegetables also help promote a healthy digestive tract.

Five Points to Remember

- Eat five servings of fruits and vegetables a day!
- Eat at least one vitamin A rich selection every day!
- Eat at least one vitamin C rich selection every day!
- Eat at least one high fiber selection every day!
- Eat cabbage family vegetables several times each week!

---

1. fiber: a substance that moves food and waste quickly through intestines.
2. cholesterol: a substance that can block arteries, leading to heart disease.
3. nutrients: substances in food that nourish, or promote growth.

How close are you to meeting the 5 a Day Goal?

How many servings of fruits or vegetables did you eat yesterday:

At breakfast? _____

At lunch? _____

For a snack? _____

At dinner? _____

For dessert? _____

Total = _____

Does your total equal the Goal of 5?

5 a day . . . it may be easier than you think!

Morning

Drink a glass of juice.
Add sliced bananas or strawberries to your cereal.
Have a bowl of fruit such as melon or peaches.
Top your pancakes with fruit instead of syrup.

Snack

Nibble on some grapes.
Take along some dried fruit like raisins, apricots, prunes, or figs.
Choose a glass of juice.
Keep cut raw vegetables in the refrigerator.

Lunch

Have a salad or soup that has vegetables.
Add zucchini, carrot, or celery sticks to your brown bag lunch.
Eat a piece of fruit like an apple or an orange.

Add lettuce, sprouts, and tomatoes to your sandwich.

Dinner

Add vegetables to your main dish such as broccoli to your pasta or casserole.
Add raw vegetables or fruit to your green salad.
Use fruits as a garnish on main dishes.
Order extra vegetables when you are eating out.

Dessert

Liven up a plain dessert with fresh fruit.
Top frozen yogurt with pineapple or papaya.
Add chopped fruit or berries to muffins, cakes, or cookies.

Check-in What questions might you ask about how fruits and vegetables help keep you healthy? Has the pamphlet answered any of the questions you asked on page 24?

All Fruits and Vegetables supply a variety of nutrients!
Some are especially good sources of vitamins A and C, and most contain fiber.

Fruits	Vitamin A	Vitamin C	Fiber
Apple			■
Apricots (3)	●		■
Banana			■
Figs (2)			●
Grapes (1 cup)			■
Grapefruit (1/2)		●	■
Kiwi Fruit		●	■
Nectarine			■
Orange		●	■
Peach			■
Pear			●
Plums (2)			■
Prunes (4)			●
1/2 cup serving			
Cantaloupe	●	●	■
Honeydew		■	
Papaya	■	●	
Pineapple			■
Raisins (1/4 cup)			■
Raspberries		■	■
Strawberries		●	■
Watermelon (1 cup)		■	
Juices 3/4 cup			
Orange Juice		●	
Grapefruit Juice		●	
Tomato Juice		●	

Vegetables 1/2 cup cooked	Vitamin A	Vitamin C	Fiber
Asparagus		■	■
Beans, Green			■
Bok Choy	●	■	■
Broccoli	■	●	■
Brussels Sprouts		●	■
Cabbage		■	■
Carrots	●		■
Cauliflower		●	■
Chili Peppers (1/4 cup)	●	●	
Corn			■
Dried Peas and Beans			●
Eggplant			■
Green Pepper		●	
Greens [1]	●	■	■
Lettuce (1 cup fresh)			
Spinach	●	■	■
Romaine	■		
Red and green looseleaf	■		
Iceberg			
Okra			■
Peas, Green			■
Potato (1 medium baked)		■	■
Spinach	●		■
Squash, Winter	●		■
Sweet Potato	●		■
Tomatoes (1)	■	■	■
Zucchini			■

■ These selections supply at least 25% of the U.S. Recommended Daily Allowances (RDA) for vitamins A or C or at least 1–3 grams of dietary fiber per serving.

● These selections supply at least 50% of the U.S. RDA for vitamins A or C or at least 4 grams of dietary fiber per serving.

1: Values are averages calculated using beet and mustard greens, swiss chard, dandelion, kale and turnip greens. These foods are part of the cabbage family.

Sources for Table: USDA Handbook No 8; Produce Marketing Association; and the Minnesota Nutrition Data System.

Final Check-in

As a purpose for reading, you jotted down some questions about nutrition information you wanted to learn about fruits and vegetables. Which of your questions, if any, were answered?

After You Read

A. Comprehension Check Check whether each statement is **True** or **False**.

True   **False**

_____   _____   **1.** Eat only 2 to 3 fruits and vegetables a day.

_____   _____   **2.** Choose foods that are low in fat.

_____   _____   **3.** Vitamin pills are just as good as fresh fruits and vegetables.

_____   _____   **4.** Fruits and vegetables are high in cholesterol.

_____   _____   **5.** Fruits and vegetables have no effect on heart disease.

_____   _____   **6.** Cancer may be related to too much fat and not enough fiber.

_____   _____   **7.** A balanced diet includes food from all five basic food groups.

_____   _____   **8.** Dried fruits aren't good for you.

_____   _____   **9.** The best diet is low in saturated fat and high in fiber.

_____   _____   **10.** Too much cholesterol can harm your arteries.

B. Revisit the Reading Strategy Consider what you knew before and after reading the pamphlet. Answer these questions on your own or with a partner.

1. What new food fact did you learn that may change what you eat?
2. Which topic added information to what you already know?
3. What do you still want to know more about?

C. Think Beyond the Reading In order to truly adopt a healthy diet, most of us need support from friends and loved ones. If we begin to fall back into poor eating habits, they can remind us to get back on track. With a partner or a small group, discuss the need for support. Is support important to you? How can you provide support to others?

Think About It: Apply Information

You have just read a pamphlet that was full of information about healthy eating. When you read informative materials, you may want to apply some of the facts you learn to your own life. This is called **applying information.**

A. Look at Applying Information

Suppose you decided to add more fiber to your diet. Turn back to page 27. What two high-fiber foods would you like to try?

_____   _____

You might have chosen any two foods that have a symbol in the column headed "Fiber" on the chart.

B. Practice

1. For one day, make a list of all the fruits and vegetables that you eat.
2. At the end of the day, fill in the chart below. If you ate fewer than five fruits and vegetables over the course of the day, consider adding more to your diet. Check the chart on page 27 for ideas on what to try. Add those choices to your chart using a different color ink. Then try adding those choices to your diet in the next few days.

Meal	Fruits	Vegetables
Breakfast		
A.M. snack		
Lunch		
P.M. snack		
Dinner		
Late snack		

Write About It: Fill in a KWL Chart

A KWL chart is a way to organize information about a subject you will read about. *K* stands for "What I **K**now," *W* stands for "What I **W**ant to Find Out," and *L* stands for "What I **L**earned." Here is the top of a KWL chart. Copy the headings on separate paper.

K	W	L
What I Know	What I Want to Find Out	What I Learned

A. **Prewriting** "On the Go with Good Food" tells how you can eat well when you are on the go, spending a lot of time in a car or bus. Before you read the article, fill in parts *K* and *W* of your KWL chart to organize your prior knowledge and to set a purpose for reading. Under *K,* fill in what you *already know* about how to get good food when you are on the go. Under *W,* write what you *want to find out* about this topic. Then read the article.

> **On the Go with Good Food**
>
> Whether you go from place to place by bus or car, resist buying candy bars! You can just as easily buy fruits or vegetables, even at convenience stores.
>
> Buy fruits and vegetables that you can eat easily. Try apples, peaches, pears, celery, cherry tomatoes, cherries, strawberries, and grapes. Most stores will wash a piece of fruit for you. Or you can buy dried fruits that don't need to be washed. These include prunes, raisins, apricots, figs, and dates.
>
> For a drink, buy real fruit juice in a can or box instead of sodas or coffee. Grab a can and run to the express check-out line!
>
> Fruits, vegetables, and fruit drinks are a quick, nutritious snack wherever you are.

B. **Writing** Under *L* in your chart, write what you *learned* that you didn't already know before you read the article.

Life Skill: A Closer Look at a Food Chart

Charts are designed to show information in an easy-to-read format. When you read a chart, first read the title. Then read the column headings and the row headings. These will help you understand what the chart is about.

To find specific information on a chart, read down the columns and across the rows. For example, according to the chart below, what substance is found in 1/2 cup of cooked green beans?

_____

If you said *fiber,* you are correct.

Nutrients in Fruits and Vegetables

Fruits	Vitamin A	Vitamin C	Fiber	Vegetables 1/2 cup cooked	Vitamin A	Vitamin C	Fiber
Apple			■	Asparagus		■	■
Apricots (3)	●		■	Beans, Green			■
Banana			■	Bok Choy	●	■	■
Figs (2)			●	Broccoli	■	●	■
Grapes (1 cup)			■	Brussels Sprouts		●	■
Grapefruit (1/2)		●	■	Cabbage		■	■
Kiwi Fruit		●	■	Carrots	●		■
Nectarine			■	Cauliflower		●	■
Orange		●	■	Chili Peppers (1/4 cup)	●	●	
Peach			■	Corn			■
Pear			●	Dried Peas and Beans			●
Plums (2)			■	Eggplant			■
Prunes (4)			●	Green Pepper		■	

■ These selections supply at least 25% of the U.S. Recommended Daily Allowances (RDA) for vitamins A or C or at least 1–3 grams of dietary fiber per serving.

● These selections supply at least 50% of the U.S. RDA for vitamins A or C or at least 4 grams of dietary fiber per serving.

Practice

1. Name one vegetable that contains vitamins A and C, and fiber. _____

2. Would you eat an apple to get a lot of fiber? _____

3. What substances are found in carrots? _____

4. Can you get more than 4 grams of fiber from a serving of cabbage? _____

5. Name two fruits that contain vitamin C. _____

Lesson 3

LEARNING GOALS

Strategy: Predict content
Reading: Read an article
Skill: Understand cause and effect
Writing: Create a chart
Life Skill: Fill in a medical history form

Before You Read

Have you ever had food poisoning? Do you know someone who has? In this lesson, you will be reading an article titled "How to Avoid Food that Makes You Sick." Try to **predict** the **content** of the article, or guess what will be in it. List some kinds of information you think will be in an article about avoiding food poisoning.

_____

_____

_____

Preview the Reading

Preview the article by reading the title and its three main headings. Look at the chart title. The article will contain many facts to help you understand food-borne illness. Predict some of the ways the article will give to *prevent* food poisoning.

▶ **Use the Strategy**

As you read this article about food poisoning, think about the types of information you predicted on page 32. Were some of your predictions correct?

How to Avoid Food that Makes You Sick

Linda C. Hadfield, M.S., R.D., L.D.

You see it in the news every day. Several people died from eating improperly cooked hamburgers. Many people in several states suffered from food poisoning after eating ice cream. One person became ill from eating fruit tainted[1] with a pesticide[2] Still another fell victim to vegetables laden with salmonella [sal ma NEL la] from a cutting board. It's enough to make you . . . well, sick.

Instead of living in fear of eating certain kinds of food, what can we do to reduce the risk of eating something that could be harmful? Here are some tips to reduce your risk of food-borne illness.

---

1. **tainted:** infected, spoiled.
2. **pesticide:** a chemical used to kill pests such as rodents or insects.

Tips to Reduce Your Risk of Food-borne Illness

- Keep hot foods hot. Cook meat, poultry, and fish to an internal temperature of at least 160 degrees Fahrenheit.
- Keep cold foods cold. Put a thermometer in your refrigerator. It should read 40 degrees F or less. Your freezer should be 0 degrees F or less.
- Raw meat and poultry should be wrapped securely in a sealed plastic bag or in a container. They should be placed on the lower shelf so they do not leak and contaminate other foods and surfaces.
- Use or freeze fresh meat, fish, or poultry within a day or two of purchase.
- Keep your refrigerator clean. Remove spoiled food and clean up any spills. Keep cooked and raw food separate.
- Thaw frozen foods in the refrigerator.
- Marinate[3] meats in the refrigerator. If you wish to use the marinade for a sauce or to brush on cooked meat, bring it to a rolling boil first.
- Wash your hands thoroughly before preparing foods. And afterward—especially when working with eggs, poultry, and meat—wash hands again. Wash all kitchen surfaces and utensils used.
- If you are sick, stay out of the kitchen.

Before you began to read this article, you predicted what types of information you would find. Which of your predictions are correct so far? What do you expect to find in the next sections?

◀ Check-in

Pass the E. coli [CO lie] 0157:H7, Please

In the spring of 1993, a 2-year-old boy ate a fast-food hamburger contaminated with a deadly bacterium—E. coli 0157:H7. He seemed fine when he left the restaurant. But a few weeks later, he was dead.

Several hundred other unsuspecting customers also ate hamburgers made from the same batch of contaminated meat, at this same restaurant. What has become the most widely publicized case of food contamination with the bacteria, E. coli 0157:H7, resulted in at least three deaths and more than

3. **marinate:** soak in vinegar or wine, spices, and herbs.

100 hospitalizations. It all could have been avoided with proper food safety techniques.

According to health officials, the hamburgers in question may have been heated to only 120 degrees—far below the recommended temperature of 160 degrees. Improper hand-washing techniques also were to blame. As many as 60 people were exposed to the bacteria indirectly by coming in contact with someone who had eaten the tainted meat.

As a result of this outbreak, the federal government has issued this guideline for cooking ground beef: Cook hamburgers until the center is gray or brown and the juices run clear. If you like your meat pink, order a steak. Since E. coli is usually found on the meat's surface, you still can eat a steak that is pink in the middle. Hamburger, however, is ground. The surface meat is mixed throughout the batch, as are the bacteria. Cooking the hamburger to an internal temperature of 160 degrees, however, kills the E. coli.

Though not as widely reported, this strain of E. coli also resides in raw milk, improperly processed apple cider, and contaminated water. For your own protection, the health department advises drinking only pasteurized milk, treated water, and pasteurized cider. If you buy cider at a roadside stand, for example, heat it to at least 160 degrees (a slow simmer where steam starts to rise from the pan) before serving or refrigerating.

Something Smells Fishy

It used to be called "brain food." Now, reports of fish poisoning have been steadily trickling through the media. Contamination of fish with ciguatera [see GWA ter a] is increasing. By some estimates, it is the most common illness associated with fish consumption in the United States. Ciguatera is produced by a tiny plant that lives on coral reefs. Small fish eat these plants. Larger fish eat the smaller fish; then you eat the bigger fish. Food and Drug Administration (FDA) sources say we shouldn't stop eating fish. However, it's best to stay away from the ones that are most likely to be contaminated: fish that live in warm waters near coral reefs, such as grouper, snapper, amberjack, and barracuda.

When buying fish, take a whiff. Fresh fish should not smell like fish or ammonia. It should have a faint odor, almost like cucumbers.

If you like to fish, make sure that the waters are approved for harvest. If you're not sure, contact your local health department.

 Final Check-in

Before you read this article, you predicted what content you would find. Were your predictions correct? Do you have a better understanding of food-borne illnesses?

The chart below lists five types of bacteria that cause food poisoning. It gives the symptoms, the food sources, and ways to prevent each type of food poisoning.

Food Poisoning Facts

Type	Symptoms	Foods	Prevention
Campylobacter [kam pi lo BAK ter]	Diarrhea, abdominal pain, nausea, vomiting, fever, and cramps. Occurs 2 to 10 days after eating.	Meat, poultry, eggs, unpasteurized dairy products, fish, shellfish, and untreated water.	Cook meat, poultry, and eggs thoroughly; wash hands and work surfaces before and after contact with raw meat and poultry.
Salmonella [sal mo NEL la]	Nausea, vomiting, diarrhea, cramps, fever, and headache. Occurs 6 to 48 hours after eating.	Meat, poultry, eggs, and unpasteurized dairy products.	Same as campylobacter. Don't let foods sit at room temperature for over 2 hours; don't drink unpasteurized milk.
Staphylococcus [staf a lo KAH kus]	Vomiting and diarrhea, occasionally weakness and dizziness. Occurs 30 minutes to 8 hours after eating.	Cooked meat and poultry; meat, poultry, potato and egg salads, creme-filled pastries.	Wash hands and utensils before preparing food; don't let food sit at room temperature for over 2 hours.
Listeria monocytogenes [lis TER ee a mon o si TOJ a nus]	Fever, headache, nausea, and vomiting. Occurs 3 to 21 days after eating.	Soft cheeses, ice cream, prepared salads, seafoods.	Be cautious in food handling; cook seafoods thoroughly.
E. coli [E. CO lie]	Bloody diarrhea, severe abdominal cramps. Occurs 3 to 9 days after eating.	Raw ground beef, unpasteurized milk, cheeses.	Cook beef thoroughly until juices run clear.

After You Read

A. Comprehension Check

1. To avoid food poisoning, cook meat, poultry, and fish to an internal temperature of
   (1) 106 degrees Fahrenheit (F)
   (2) 120 degrees F
   (3) 140 degrees F
   (4) 160 degrees F

2. When cooking hamburger, be sure the meat
   (1) is cooked until it is pink inside
   (2) is gray or brown in the center
   (3) is brown on the outside
   (4) is cooked the day you buy it

3. Since ciguatera is found in coral reefs, it is a good idea to avoid eating
   (1) all fish
   (2) fish caught in rivers
   (3) fish caught in warm waters
   (4) fish caught in fresh water lakes

4. When you buy fresh chicken, you should
   (1) cook it within a week
   (2) store it separately from any cooked chicken
   (3) always put it in the freezer
   (4) store it on the top shelf of the refrigerator

B. Revisit the Reading Strategy
Look at the predictions you listed before you read the article. Which of these predictions were actually in the article?

Compare your prediction list with what you found in the article. How many matches are there? _____

If you had questions that weren't answered in the article, think about where you could find the answers.

C. Think Beyond the Reading
Think about these questions and discuss them with a partner. Answer the questions in writing if you wish.

1. What shopping and cooking habits can you change to better protect yourself and your family from food poisoning?
2. The federal government requires that all fresh meat be sold with "safe handling" guidelines printed on the package. Do you think this is a good idea? Why or why not?

Think About It: Understand Cause and Effect

When things happen in our lives, we often ask, "Why?" We are looking for the **cause**—the reason why something happened. A cause leads to an **effect**—what happened, or the outcome.

A. Look at Cause and Effect

Cause ➡️ **Effect**

A woman eats meat contaminated with E. coli.

The woman becomes seriously ill.

Cue words such as *since, because, therefore, as a result,* and *consequently* are often clues to cause and effect.

Look for the cause and the effect in these examples. Fill in the blanks as shown in Example 1. Examples 1 and 2 contain cue words. There is no cue word in Example 3.

Example 1: Two boys drink untreated mountain stream water. As a result, two days later, they become nauseous and feverish.

Cause ➡️ **Cue words** ➡️ **Effect**

They drink untreated water   as a result   they get sick

Example 2: In a hurry to make dinner, a man forgets to wash the knife he used to cut raw chicken. He uses the same knife to cut vegetables. Consequently, a few days later, the family gets sick.

Cause ➡️ **Cue word** ➡️ **Effect**

_____   _____   _____

The cause is using a tainted knife. The effect is the family getting sick. The cue word is *consequently.*

Example 3: A woman suffers from diarrhea, vomiting, cramps, and fever. The day before, she had eaten salmonella-tainted eggs.

Cause ➡️ **Effect**

_____   _____

Notice that in this example, the effect is stated first. The cause is eating tainted eggs and the effect is becoming very ill. There was no cue word.

B. Practice For each item, underline the cause with <u>one line</u> and the effect with <u>two lines.</u> (Circle) the cue word if there is one.

1. Charlie baked the chicken to an internal temperature of 160 degrees in order to completely kill harmful bacteria.

2. When meat is not cooked thoroughly, *E. coli* can remain alive in the meat.

3. Adnan sets his refrigerator at 40 degrees; consequently, food in his refrigerator does not become tainted.

4. Liz learned that fish living in warm waters near coral reefs are most likely to be contaminated; therefore, she avoids eating those fish.

5. Employees at a local restaurant did not wash their hands before handling food and dishes. They contaminated the food with bacteria from their hands.

6. Pasteurization kills bacteria; as a result, pasteurized milk is safer to drink.

7. Sarah washes fresh fruits and vegetables thoroughly because they may have been sprayed with pesticides.

▶ **Talk About It**
One of your best weapons against food poisoning may be asking questions. Think of questions you could ask the people who sell you meat, fish, and dairy products. What questions could you ask at restaurants? With a partner or a small group, brainstorm a list of questions that can help ensure that the food you buy is fresh and untainted.

Write About It: Create a Chart

In Lesson 2, you read a food chart. In this lesson, you have read a chart containing information on food poisoning. **Charts** present information arranged in columns and rows. In the sample chart below, the column headings are categories of food-handling procedures. The row headings are specific types of food. To fill in the chart, write appropriate information in the box under a column heading and across from a row heading. For example, in the box under the column heading "Proper Storage" and across from "hamburger," you might write "wrap securely" and "store at 40° or cooler."

Create a chart that you can hang up in your kitchen to remind yourself of the safest way to handle different kinds of foods.

A. **Prewriting** Use the sample chart here to practice writing information in a chart.

Food Handling Chart

Foods	Proper Storage	Preparation Tips	Internal Temperature
hamburger	Wrap securely Store at 40° F or cooler	Cook until center is gray or brown	160° F
frozen fish			
raw chicken			

B. **Writing** Now create your own food-handling chart on separate paper. You may change the headings on the chart to include foods you eat regularly. Add any information from this lesson or from any other sources you find helpful.

▶ **Save your draft.** At the end of this unit, you will choose one of your drafts to work with further.

Life Skill: Fill in a Medical History Form

When people are admitted to a hospital or visit a doctor for the first time, they are usually asked for their complete medical history. This includes past illnesses and surgeries, current allergies, and medicines being taken. It is important to give complete and accurate information on these forms.

Practice The form below lists some of the information commonly requested on a medical history form. You can make up answers if you don't want to share private information.

Medical History

Name:_____ Date:_____

1. **Allergies** (Medicine, Food, Environment)		2. **Medications Taken Regularly**	
Allergy	Type of Reaction	Name of Medicine	Dosage/Frequency

3. Major Illnesses
List all major illnesses and approximate dates (for example: heart disease, kidney disease, diabetes, hypertension).

Illness	Date	Illness	Date

4. Surgical History
List the approximate date of all surgeries. State any problems related to the surgery (for example: infection, bleeding, or reaction to anesthesia).

Type of Surgery	Date	Problems

Writing Skills Mini-Lesson: Fixing Sentence Fragments

A **complete sentence** contains a complete thought. It must have a **subject** (who or what the sentence is about) and a **verb** (what the subject does or is). A simple sentence is also called an **independent clause,** because it stands alone. A **sentence fragment** does not contain a complete thought. It cannot stand alone. Here are two kinds of fragments and two ways to fix each one.

1. **Fragment:** Candy, donuts, and potato chips.

   This fragment has no verb. It does not make sense all by itself. To fix it, you must make the fragment into a complete sentence. Add a verb and any other words needed to make a complete thought.

   - Candy, donuts, and potato chips **are bad for your health.**
   - **You should avoid** candy, donuts, and potato chips.

2. **Fragment:** If you want to be healthy

   Although this fragment has a subject *(you)* and a verb *(want)*, it is not a complete thought. It is a **dependent clause.** To fix it, you can attach it to an independent clause to make the sentence complete. Add a comma after the dependent clause if it comes first.

   - If you want to be healthy, **you must eat right.**
   - **You must eat right** if you want to be healthy.

Practice The paragraph below contains several fragments. On your own paper, rewrite the paragraph and fix the fragments. Add any words needed to make complete thoughts.

> Parents need to feed their children. Healthy food. Unfortunately, too many children. Junk food. They prefer potato chips and cola. Carrots and milk. If they eat only junk food. Get sick often. What can parents do? For one thing. Only healthy food in the home. It is wise to start. Good habits. Before children are old enough for school.

▶ Unit 1 Review

Reading Review

This reading is about Pat's problems with her diet. Read it and answer the questions that follow.

Pat Struggles with Her Diet

In March, Pat threw her box of chocolates into the Dumpster. She was determined to change her eating habits and win back her daughter Rachel's respect. But she had no idea how hard it would be to eat healthy foods and avoid junk food.

One month later, Pat felt as if she were punishing herself. For thirty days she had eaten hardly any high-fat foods—no candy, chips, or cookies. Instead she had eaten fruits, fruit juices, and plain vegetables. She had studied calorie charts. As a result, for main courses she had eaten chicken more often than beef. She had avoided fatty meats such as hot dogs completely. Her body felt better and she had more energy. But Pat was miserable. The six pounds she had lost could not stop her from feeling deprived all the time.

Pat almost quit the diet. But then she had an idea. "Maybe just one treat a week," she thought. "One really delicious treat." She decided to try it. It was better than quitting altogether, Pat reasoned. She promised herself she would never again eat chocolates every night.

The next Friday, Pat shopped for the weekend. She filled her cart with the nutritious foods she had gotten used to buying. Then she stopped at the store bakery. She chose a small piece of double chocolate cake. "This is my reward," she said to the bakery worker. Pat smiled. "This will keep me going all week!"

Check whether the following statements are **True** or **False**.

	True	False	
	_____	_____	**1.** This story mainly deals with the tensions between Pat and her daughter, Rachel.
	_____	_____	**2.** Pat was satisfied with her first diet plan because she felt better and lost some weight.
	_____	_____	**3.** Pat was miserable because she couldn't lose any weight.
	_____	_____	**4.** Pat ate fruit and plain vegetables because they were low in fat.
	_____	_____	**5.** Pat was applying calorie information when she chose a piece of chocolate cake.
	_____	_____	**6.** It is hard for Pat to avoid high fat foods.
	_____	_____	**7.** Pat solved her problem by eating chocolates every night.

Writing Process

In Unit 1, you wrote two first drafts. Choose the piece below that you would like to work with further. You will revise, edit, and make a final copy of this draft.

_____ your paragraph on Pat one year later (page 22)

_____ your food-handling chart (page 40)

Find the first draft you chose. Then turn to page 160 in this book. Follow steps 3, 4, and 5 in the Writing Process to create a final draft.

As you revise, check your draft for these specific points:

Paragraph: Did you write a topic sentence that sums up the main point of the paragraph? Did you remember to turn any sentence fragments into complete sentences?

Chart: Did you check each tip to be sure it will help you avoid food poisoning?

Unit 2 Get That Job!

An important goal for most people is to have a secure and satisfying job. We hear many news stories about workers who have been laid off and are looking for work. We also hear a lot of information about new jobs that are opening up now or that will open up in the future. Whether looking for a first job, trying to replace a lost job, or looking for a better job, we must all prepare ourselves to take advantage of new jobs that become available. Unit 2 is full of practical ideas you can use when seeking a job.

Be an Active Reader

As you read the selections in this unit

- Put a question mark (?) by things you do not understand.
- <u>Underline</u> words you do not know. Try to use context clues to figure them out.

After you read each selection in this unit

- Reread sections you marked with a question mark (?). If they still do not make sense, discuss them with a partner or your instructor.
- Look at words you underlined. Discuss any words you still don't understand with a partner or your instructor, or look them up in a dictionary.

Lesson 4

LEARNING GOALS

Strategy: Visualize
Reading: Read a story
Skill: Understand cause and effect
Writing: Write about a dream job
Life Skill: Interpret want ads

Before You Read

"Easy Job, Good Wages" is a story about using newspaper want ads to find jobs. Although the events in this story happened many years ago, you can still find the same kind of misleading information in want ads today.

Before you read the story, answer these questions:

- Can you think of a job that is both easy to do and pays good wages?
- Now **visualize,** or picture in your mind, what it would be like to have the job in question 1.
- Next, can you think of a job that would be hard to do?
- Visualize what it would be like to do the hard job.

Preview the Reading

To preview the story, look at the title and the pictures. Then read the first sentence in each paragraph. This will give you a sense of where the story is going. As you read each sentence, try to imagine what else will be described in each paragraph.

Use the Strategy

In this story, the author describes a very unpleasant job experience he had. Pay attention to the details that the author uses to describe himself and his job. Picture these details as you read.

Easy Job, Good Wages

Jesus Colon [hay SOOS   co LONE]

This happened early in 1919. We were both out of work, my brother and I. He got up earlier to look for a job. When I woke up, he was already gone. So I dressed, went out and bought a copy of the *New York World* and turned its pages until I got to the "Help Wanted—Unskilled" section of the paper. After much reading and rereading the same columns, my attention was held by a small advertisement. It read: "Easy job. Good wages. No experience necessary." This was followed by a number and street on the west side of lower Manhattan. It sounded like the job I was looking for. Easy job. Good wages. Those four words revolved in my brain as I was traveling toward the address indicated in the advertisement. Easy job. Good wages. Easy Job. Good wages. Easy . . .

The place consisted of a small front office and a large loft. On the floor of the loft I noticed a series of large galvanized tubs half filled with water. Out of the water protruded[1] the necks of many

---

1. protrude: stick out.

bottles of various sizes and shapes. Around these tubs there were a number of workers, male and female, sitting on small wooden benches. All had their hands in the water of the tub, the left hand holding a bottle and with the thumbnail of the right hand scratching the labels.

The foreman found a vacant stool for me around one of the tubs of water. I asked why a penknife or a small safety razor could not be used instead of the thumbnail to take off the old labels from the bottles. I was expertly informed that knives or razors would scratch the glass. This would lower the value of the bottles when they were to be sold.

I sat down and started to use my thumbnail on one bottle. The water had somewhat softened the transparent mucilage[2] used to attach the label to the bottle. But the softening did not work out uniformly somehow. There were always pieces of label that for some obscure reason remained affixed to the bottles. It was on those pieces of labels tenaciously[3] fastened to the bottles that my right hand thumbnail had to work overtime. As the minutes passed I noticed that the coldness of the water started to pass from my hand to my body. This gave me body shivers that I tried to conceal with the greatest of effort from those sitting beside me. My hands became deadly clean. Tiny little wrinkles started to show, especially at the tips of my fingers. Sometimes I stopped a few seconds from scratching the bottles, to open and close my fists in rapid movements in order to bring blood to my hands. But almost as soon as I placed them in the water they became deathly pale again.

◀ Check-in

But these were minor details compared with what was happening to the thumb of my right hand. For a delicate, boyish thumb, it was growing by the minute into a full blown tomato colored finger. It was the only part of my right hand remaining blood red. I started to look at the workers' thumbs. I noticed that

2. **mucilage:** glue.
3. **tenaciously:** stubbornly.

Now that you know what Colon is experiencing, imagine what the hands of the whole group of workers might look like. Read on to see if your image is correct.

these particular fingers on their right hands were unusually developed. They each had a thick layer of corn-like surface at the top of their right thumb. The nails on their thumbs looked coarser and smaller than on the other fingers. Thumb and nail had become one and the same thing—a primitive unnatural human tool especially developed to detach hard pieces of labels from wet bottles sunk in galvanized tubs.

After a couple of hours I had a feeling that my thumbnail was going to leave my finger and jump into the cold water of the tub. A numb pain slowly began to be felt coming from my right thumb.

Then I began to feel such pain as if coming from a finger bigger than all of my body.

After three hours of this I decided to quit fast. I told the foreman so, showing him my swollen finger. He figured I had earned 69 cents at 23 cents an hour.

Early in the evening I met my brother in our furnished room. We started to exchange experiences of our job hunting for the day. "You know what?" my brother started. "Early in the morning I went to work where they take labels off old bottles—with your right hand thumbnail . . . Somewhere on the west side of lower Manhattan. I only stayed a couple of hours. 'Easy job . . . Good wages . . .' they said. The person who wrote that ad must have had a great sense of humor." And we both had a hearty laugh that evening when I told my brother that I also went to work at that same place later in the day.

Now when I see ads reading "Easy job. Good wages," I just smile an ancient, tired, knowing smile.

▶ **Final Check-in**
As you read the story, did you visualize the experience of Jesus Colon? Think about the mental pictures you created. Which one is the most dramatic?

After You Read

A. Comprehension Check

1. What words caught Colon's attention as he was looking in the want ad section of the newspaper?

   _____

2. What kind of work environment did Colon see when he entered the work room? Visualize it before you answer.

   _____

3. Do you think the workers had any choice about how they did the job? Why or why not?

   _____

4. How could this experience help the two brothers as they continue to search in the want ads for jobs?

   _____

B. Revisit the Reading Strategy
Recall the mental pictures you formed as you read "Easy Job, Good Wages." Then picture how you would change the working conditions of this job. First review how the job was done. Then think of what could be done to make this job less harmful to the workers' hands. Share your ideas with the rest of the group.

C. Think Beyond the Reading
Think about these questions and discuss them with a partner. Answer the questions in writing if you wish.

1. Do you think it is important for employers to establish strict safety measures for their workers? Why or why not?

2. What qualities make a boss a good person to work for? Discuss both good and bad qualities you have observed in bosses. Discuss how these qualities affect the workers.

Think About It: Understand Cause and Effect

In Lesson 3, you learned that the **cause** is the reason why something happened, and the **effect** is the outcome, or what happened. Keep in mind this summary of cause and effect:

Cause ➡ **Effect**
the reason why   what happened

Tip Remember that sometimes the cause is stated first. Other times the effect is stated first.

A. Review Cause and Effect

The following example from the story shows a cause and an effect:

▶ There were always pieces of label that for some obscure reason remained affixed to the bottles. It was on those pieces of labels tenaciously fastened to the bottles that my right hand thumbnail had to work overtime.

The effect is that Colon's thumb had to work overtime.

What causes his right thumb to work overtime? _____

Pieces of label that stuck to the bottles caused the extra work.

B. Practice Read each passage from the story. Write the cause and the effect on the lines provided.

1. ▶ This happened early in 1919. We were both out of work, my brother and I. He got up earlier to look for a job. When I woke up, he was already gone. So I dressed, went out and bought a copy of the *New York World* and turned its pages until I got to the "Help Wanted—Unskilled" section of the paper.

   cause _____

   effect _____

2. ▶ As the minutes passed I noticed that the coldness of the water started to pass from my hand to my body. This gave me body shivers that I tried to conceal with the greatest of effort from those sitting beside me.

cause _____

effect _____

3. ▶ But the softening did not work out uniformly somehow. There were always pieces of label that for some obscure reason remained affixed to the bottles.

cause _____

effect _____

4. ▶ Then I began to feel such pain as if coming from a finger bigger than all of my body. After three hours of this I decided to quit fast. I told the foreman so, showing him my swollen finger.

cause _____

effect _____

5. ▶ The nails on their thumbs looked coarser and smaller than on the other fingers. Thumb and nail had become one and the same thing—a primitive unnatural human tool especially developed to detach hard pieces of labels from wet bottles sunk in galvanized tubs.

cause _____

effect _____

▶ **Talk About It**

In your own words, tell what happened to Jesus Colon. How did this story begin? What events led to his decision to quit? What was the surprising and amusing ending to this tale? Tell the story to a partner or to your instructor.

Write About It: Write About Your Dream Job

The job described in "Easy Job, Good Wages" is no one's idea of a dream job. But what *is* a dream job? What job would you most like to have? Think about your dream job. Let your imagination flow. In this activity, you will write a paragraph describing your dream job.

In Lesson 1 you learned that a **paragraph** is a group of sentences with one main idea and several supporting details. The **main idea** is the most important point. It is stated in a **topic sentence.** The **supporting details** explain, or support, the main idea.

The topic sentence—which states the main idea—is in heavy type in the paragraph below. Notice that the writer tells many details about the job of landscaper. Your paragraph does not have to be this long.

My Dream Job

   My dream job is to be an outdoor landscaper. To qualify for a job, it would help me to go to a technical school. But if I can't do that, I can get a job working for a landscape company and learn on the job. The hours can be very long in the spring, summer, and fall. Work starts as soon as possible after sunrise. The pay would start around seven dollars an hour. At first, I would probably just be digging the holes for plants and tilling the soil to remove rocks and weeds. Later, I hope to actually design and plant things. I imagine my routine would start with meeting the rest of the crew at the company headquarters, getting my orders and tools, and going with the crew to the job site. After working all morning, I would need a break in the shade. Then I would dig, haul rocks, or plant until quitting time. Then we would return to headquarters with the tools.

A. Prewriting Before you write your paragraph, think about what your dream job is. Then fill out this information sheet with details about your dream job. Remember, this is a dream job—add whatever details you'd like to have in a job.

What is the job title? _____

How many years of school do you need? _____

What kind of training should you have? _____

_____

What kind of experience is needed? _____

_____

What are your hours? _____ What is your salary? _____

What do you actually do on the job? _____

_____

_____

What are some everyday routines of the job? _____

_____

_____

B. Writing On separate paper, write a topic sentence stating the main idea of your paragraph. This sentence should state what your dream job is. Then write sentences with details about your dream job. Use the information sheet you filled in above.

▶ **Save your draft.** At the end of this unit, you will choose one of your drafts to work with further.

Life Skill: Interpret Want Ads

An important job-search skill is the ability to interpret want ads. Newspaper want ads use **abbreviations,** or shortened forms of words. Test your ability to read abbreviations. How many of these do you know?

Some Want Ad Abbreviations					
aft.	afternoon	flex.	flexible	perm.	permanent
appt.	appointment	F/T	full-time	P/T	part-time
ASAP	as soon as possible	hrs.	hours	refs.	references
attn.	attention	immed.	immediately	req.	required
eve.	evening	lic.	license	temp.	temporary
exc.	excellent	morn.	morning	trans.	transportation
exp.	experience	nec.	necessary	w/	with

Try reading this want ad. To figure out the abbreviations, ask yourself what makes sense or what word the letters look like.

Receptionist/Secretary 3 yrs. exp. w/some med. background. F/T position. Call between 10:00 A.M.–3:00 P.M. 312-555-1094

What does *exp.* mean? _____

What does *w/some* mean? _____

What might *med.* mean? _____

You were right if you answered *experience, with some,* and *medical. Medical* makes sense because it starts with the letters *med,* and it is a field in which secretaries may have experience.

Practice On your own or with a partner, read the want ads below. Underline all the abbreviations. Write their meanings on separate paper.

1. Pizza and sandwich makers. Must have own trans. F/T & P/T Call Tu. or Fri. for appt. 555-0101

2. Office work. Exp. w/computer nec. Both perm. & temp. jobs. Exc. benefits Call ASAP 555-4430

3. Attn. Exc. Job Flex. hrs. Morn, Aft.,or Eve. Begin immed. No exp. nec. Call 555-1616

4. Preschool needs tchr's. aide H.S. or G.E.D. req. Mon.– Fri. Refs. req. Call 555-1212

5. Which ad has many abbreviations but very little actual information? _____

Lesson 5

LEARNING GOALS

Strategy: Predict features
Reading: Read a job application
Skill: Locate key facts
Writing: Fill in a personal information sheet
Life Skill: Fill in a job application

Before You Read

In the short description about Kim that follows, you will learn that she is determined to find a job. Kim needs to gather information about herself for a job application. Have you ever filled in an application? Can you **predict** what questions might be asked on Kim's job application?

Which questions do you predict she will find on all applications?
Check the ones she will probably find.

_____ age   _____ national origin   _____ favorite color

_____ height   _____ years of schooling   _____ name and address

_____ weight   _____ religion   _____ most recent employer

Preview the Reading

Look at the job application on page 58. What different kinds of information are asked for? What section of the application asks the applicant for the exact dates of previous jobs?

Determined to Find a Job

Kim is 35 years old and has had only one job. She worked for a brief time as a waitress in a restaurant. Now her two children are in school all day, and she needs to add to the family income. Kim feels ready for a full-time job.

Kim wants to be a cashier. She has watched cashiers in various stores and thinks she would be a good one. She asked the manager of a grocery store for an application. Determined to find a job, she hurried home to fill it in.

Tips for Filling In a Job Application

- **Write or print in a legible manner.**
- **Use a pen, not a pencil.**
- **Carry personal information with you.** When you complete an application at a place of business, you will need to know the dates of your previous jobs, addresses and phone numbers of previous employers, and your Social Security number. Carry this information with you.
- **Give all the requested information.** Make sure you fill in all the blanks and answer all the questions. Don't skip anything.
- **Check that all numbers are correct.** Be sure you have correctly written your Social Security number and phone numbers. Include area codes.
- **Put information in the correct order.** When listing former jobs, start with the most recent.
- **Sign your name where the form asks for a signature.** Forms usually ask for your signature at or near the bottom. Always read the entire form before you sign it.

This is how Kim filled in her job application.

EMPLOYMENT APPLICATION

Name **Kim Wu**   Social Security # **485-00-0000**   Date **11-1-98**

Address **125 Concord Place**   Tel. No. Home **(101)555-0012**
   Work **none**

City **Middleton**   State **PA**   Zip **15687**

Education:	Name of School	City	No. Years Attended	Graduated		Major Course
				Yes	No	
High School	Central High School	Middleton	4	✓		business
College						
Other						
Please list any other education, training, certificates, licenses, or special skills that are related to the job for which you are applying.						

Position Wanted: **cashier**   How referred: **sign in window**

	Yes	No
Are you at least 18 years old?	✓	☐
Do you have use of a car?	☐	✓
Have you served in the military?	☐	✓

	Yes	No
Are you a U.S. Citizen?	✓	☐
If not, do you have a valid work permit?	☐	☐
Have you been convicted (found guilty) of a crime except for a misdemeanor (for example: traffic violations, speeding) in the past 5 years?	☐	✓

Part-time ☐   Full-time ✓

Days & Hours Available for Work:
Any Hour ☐   Any Day ☐

	Mon	Tues	Wed	Th	Fr	Sat	Sun
FROM	8 am	8 am	8 am	8 am	8 am		
TO	5 pm	5 pm	5 pm	5 pm	5 pm		

Previous Employment: (List in order. Start with your most recent employer first.)

Dates From	To	Name and Address of Employer	Job Title	Rate of Pay	Reason for Leaving
5/1/95	10/1/96	Name **Jones' Family Restaurant** Address **12 N. State St.** Supervisor **Lee Jones**	waitress	$5.00/hr.	family needs
		Name Address Supervisor			
		Name Address Supervisor			

References: (Not relatives or previous employers.)

Name **Mr. Prado**	Phone No. **(101)555-7643**	Occupation **teacher**
Name **Ms. Frye**	Phone No. **(101)555-7643**	Occupation **teacher**

I authorize the references listed above to give you any and all information concerning my previous employment and pertinent information they may have, personal or otherwise.

The information given herein is true to the best of my knowledge. I under-stand that falsification of this application may be just cause for dismissal.

Signature **Kim Wu**
Date **11/1/98**

After You Read

A. Comprehension Check

1. Why does Kim need a job?
   (1) to pay for child care
   (2) because her children are at school
   (3) to add to the family income
   (4) because her husband lost his
      full-time job

2. When you write your phone number
   on an application,
   (1) always write, don't print
   (2) always include the area code
   (3) just print a seven-digit number
   (4) begin with the number 800

3. How should you list your former jobs on
   an application?
   (1) List your favorite job first.
   (2) Start with your most recent employer.
   (3) Start with your very first job.
   (4) List only your most recent job.

4. What should you do before you sign the
   form?
   (1) Read the entire form.
   (2) Read only the top part of the form.
   (3) Ask the manager what to write on the
      lines.
   (4) Print, do not write, on the lines.

B. Revisit the Reading Strategy
Look back at the predictions you made on
page 56 telling what questions might be found on a job application. Did
your predictions match what you found on this application?

Why would the items below probably not be asked on applications?

1. your height
2. your favorite color
3. your religion
4. your age
5. your weight
6. your national origin

C. Think Beyond the Reading
Think about these questions and discuss them
with a partner or small group. Answer the questions in writing if you wish.

1. When filling in job applications, what personal information do
   you need to carry with you so that you can answer questions on the
   form accurately?
2. Do you make copies of all the applications you fill in? How can
   this help?

Think About It: Locate Key Facts

Employers develop job applications that will provide the information they need to make hiring decisions. In this sense, all the items on a job application are key facts.

Before you begin to fill out such a form, you should take a few minutes to read it over to be sure you understand all the questions. Notice the different sections on the form, such as the sections headed *Education* and *Previous Employment*. Look at all of the information you are asked to provide. Studying a form in this way helps you to **locate key facts.**

A. Understanding Key Terms

When filling out a job application, it is important that you read and understand all parts of the form.

Think about the meanings of the key terms from the *Education* section of the application that are underlined below.

> ▶ Please list any other <u>education</u>, <u>training</u>, <u>certificates</u>, <u>licenses</u>, or special <u>skills</u> that are related to the job for which you are applying.

This section asks you to list information about your own abilities. For example, *education* means how much school you have had. *Training* usually means a job experience in which someone specifically taught you how to do something. *Certificates* are papers that show you have completed a course of training or study. *Licenses* are papers that give you permission to do specific work, such as a cabdriver's license. *Skills* are things that you have learned to do well.

B. Practice Locating Key Facts

The manager of the grocery store had two openings for part-time cashiers.
Key facts the manager is going to look for in the application are listed below.
Look at Kim's application again. Copy Kim's responses on the lines.

1. Times and days available _____

2. Full-time or part-time _____

3. Previous employment _____

4. Education _____

5. References _____

Education:	Name of School	City	No. Years Attended	Graduated Yes	No	Major Course
High School	Central High School	Middleton	4	✓		business
College						
Other						
Please list any other education, training, certificates, licenses, or special skills that are related to the job for which you are applying.						

Position Wanted: **cashier**　　　　How referred: **sign in window**

	Yes	No		Yes	No
Are you at least 18 years old?	✓		Are you a U.S. Citizen?	✓	
Do you have use of a car?		✓	If not, do you have a valid work permit?		
Have you served in the military?		✓	Have you been convicted (found guilty) of a crime except for a misdemeanor (for example: traffic violations, speeding) in the past 5 years?		✓

Part-time ☐　Full-time ☑
Days & Hours
Available for Work:
Any Hour ☐　Any Day ☐

	Mon	Tues	Wed	Th	Fr	Sat	Sun
FROM	8 am	8 am	8 am	8 am	8 am		
TO	5 pm	5 pm	5 pm	5 pm	5 pm		

Previous Employment: (List in order. Start with your most recent employer first.)

Dates From	To	Name and Address of Employer	Job Title	Rate of Pay	Reason for Leaving
5/1/95	10/1/96	Name **Jones' Family Restaurant** Address **12 N. State St.** Supervisor **Lee Jones**	waitress	$5.00/hr.	family needs
		Name Address Supervisor			
		Name Address Supervisor			

References: (Not relatives or previous employers.)

Name	Mr. Prado	Phone No. (101)555-7643	Occupation	teacher
Name	Ms. Frye	Phone No. (101)555-7643	Occupation	teacher

I authorize the references listed above to give you any and all information concerning my previous employment and pertinent information they may have, personal or otherwise.

The information given herein is true to the best of my knowledge. I understand that falsification of this application may be just cause for dismissal.　Signature **Kim Wu**
Date **11/1/98**

▶ **Talk About It**

If you were the store manager, would you hire Kim as a part-time cashier? Why or why not? Discuss your reasons with a small group.

Write About It: Fill in a Personal Information Sheet

A personal information sheet contains information to help you thoroughly and correctly complete job application forms. An example is below. You can practice filling in this form.

Personal Information

Full Name:_____ Soc. Sec. No._____

Street Address:_____

City, State, Zip Code:_____

Area Code and Telephone Number:_____

Career Objective   (What kind of job are you looking for?)

_____

_____

Education   (Include high school, GED, college, vocational, and other training.)

School Name	Address	Years Attended From To	Graduated	Course or Major

Work Experience   (List most recent job first.)

Dates From To	Job Title	Company Name and Address	Supervisor's Name

Volunteer Experience   (List anything related to your job objective.)

_____

_____

References   (Not relatives or former employers listed above.)

Name	Address	Phone Number	Occupation

Life Skill: Fill In a Job Application

Fill in the job application below. Look back at the "Tips for Filling In a Job Application" on page 57.

EMPLOYMENT APPLICATION

Name_____ Social Security #_____ Date_____

Address_____ Tel. No. Home_____
Work_____

City_____ State_____ Zip_____

Education:	Name of School	City	No. Years Attended	Graduated Yes	No	Major Course
High School						
College						
Other						
Please list any other education, training, certificates, licenses, or special skills that are related to the job for which you are applying.						

Position Wanted:_____ How referred:_____

	Yes	No		Yes	No
Are you at least 18 years old?	☐	☐	Are you a U.S. Citizen?	☐	☐
Do you have use of a car?	☐	☐	If not, do you have a valid work permit?	☐	☐
Have you served in the military?	☐	☐	Have you been convicted (found guilty) of a crime except for a misdemeanor (for example: traffic violations, speeding) in the past 5 years?	☐	☐

Part-time ☐   Full-time ☐

Days & Hours Available for Work:
Any Hour ☐   Any Day ☐

	Mon	Tues	Wed	Th	Fr	Sat	Sun
FROM							
TO							

Previous Employment: (List in order. Start with your most recent employer first.)

Dates From	To	Name and Address of Employer	Job Title	Rate of Pay	Reason for Leaving
		Name			
		Address			
		Supervisor			
		Name			
		Address			
		Supervisor			
		Name			
		Address			
		Supervisor			

References: (Not relatives or previous employers.)

Name	Phone No.	Occupation
Name	Phone No.	Occupation

I authorize the references listed above to give you any and all information concerning my previous employment and pertinent information they may have, personal or otherwise.

The information given herein is true to the best of my knowledge. I understand that falsification of this application may be just cause for dismissal.

Signature_____

Date_____

Lesson 6

LEARNING GOALS

Strategy: Use your prior knowledge
Reading: Read an article
Skill: Identify the main idea
Writing: Write about an interesting job
Life Skill: Fill out a job network web

Before You Read

Before you read "Tips for Job Hunting," consider your **prior knowledge,** or what you already know, about job hunting. Your ideas are important. If you were asked to contribute content for this article, what would you suggest? Jot down your ideas here.

_____

_____

_____

Preview the Reading

Preview the article by reading the headings of the sections. This will tell you the main ideas in the article. Are any of them similar to the ideas you suggested on the lines above?

▶ **Use the Strategy**

As you read, compare what you know about job hunting to the main ideas in the article. What you already know, together with what you learn from the article, can help you in a job search.

Tips for Job Hunting ▬▬▬▬▬▬▬▬

Know Your Skills and Abilities

When you go job hunting, you need to think about what you have to offer an employer. Take time to recognize your strengths. What are you good at doing? What do you enjoy doing? Think of the skills that you feel employers want in a worker. All of your past jobs have helped you build your skills and abilities. For example, you may be good at typing, working on a team, using basic math, or doing small-piece assembly work. If you have been at home with children, you have also developed many skills. You'll want to be able to discuss your skills and abilities when you are talking to employers.

Brush Up Your Skills

It is important to consider what you need to do to improve your skills. Most employers want workers who can speak and understand English. They also want workers who can handle the daily reading and writing requirements of the job. Many jobs also involve basic math. You may need to brush up on your communication skills or your math skills. Your instructor or an employment specialist can help you look at how employable you are now, as well as how to develop an education plan to brush up on your skills.

Actively Search

As you begin your job search, you must find out what kinds of jobs are available. Job opportunities change. Some jobs vanish; new jobs appear. When you learn what jobs are available, you can see how your skills match the current job market.

One of the best ways to search for a job is to talk to other people. Don't try to hunt for a job all by yourself. Let your friends and relatives know you are job hunting. Personal contacts are often the best way to find a job. There are other helpful sources, such as state employment centers. At a state employment center you can talk with an employment specialist who can help you think about what kind of job you want. This person can also discuss job openings with you.

There are other ways to search for jobs besides talking with people. You can look at the want ads in newspapers, but these ads are not always the best source. Keep in mind that many jobs are not advertised in the paper. Look for signs in company windows or on neighborhood bulletin boards in libraries or grocery stores.

Most jobs will not come looking for you. It can take a lot of work to find the job you want. Be prepared to give time and energy to this task. Be prepared for some rejections. Almost everyone who has hunted for a job has felt discouraged at times. But finding a job that you really like will be worth the effort.

So far, does the article agree with what you already know about searching in different places for a job? What would you add?

◀ Check-in

Knock on the Right Doors

By now you know that you should tell people you are looking for a job so they can help you. But how do you know who to tell? How do you know who can help you? Start by learning about your network. There are more people who can help you than you might realize. Think for a moment: Who do you know? Look at the diagram below. It is an example of a typical network. Each of us is at the center of our own network, and all the people we know are in the surrounding circles. You can ask any of these people for job information.

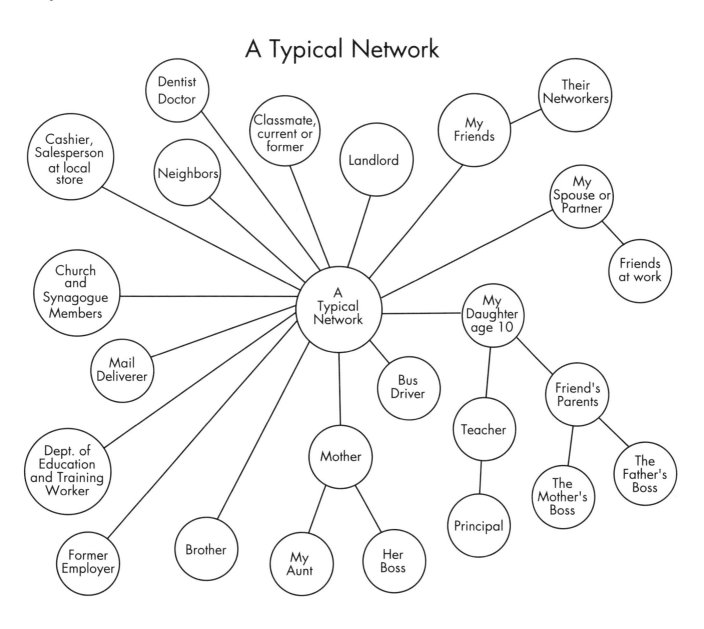

A Typical Network

Prepare for an Interview

After you have applied for a job, you may be called for an interview. Before the interview, you should do these things:

- **Get some information about the company.** Find out what they do or make. Find out who their customers are.
- **Think about questions you have about the job.** What do you need to know about the job? Do you understand what the job includes?
- **Think about what the interviewer might ask you.** Prepare answers to some questions that you might be asked.

Interview Tips

Getting Ready
- First impressions count.
- Dress appropriately. Be neat and clean. Be on time!
- Take any license or certification needed for the job.

During the Interview
- Keep eye contact with the interviewer.
- Listen carefully and answer questions as directly as possible.
- Be positive and confident but not boastful.
- Avoid negative comments about your previous employer.
- Emphasize that you are a responsible worker.
- Explain your skills that relate to the job.

At the End
- Give the interviewer any letters of recommendation.
- Ask if you can call back for the results of your interview.
- Before you leave, thank the interviewer for talking with you.

Once you have analyzed and improved your skills, searched actively, identified your job network, and prepared for interviews, you will be in a good position to get a job that is right for you.

▶ **Final Check-in**
What interview tips could you add? What people, if any, could you add to your network?

After You Read

A. Comprehension Check Check whether each statement is **True** or **False**.

True	False	
_____	_____	**1.** Answering want ads is the best way to find a job.
_____	_____	**2.** Most employers want workers who can speak and understand English.
_____	_____	**3.** Don't ask questions about the company during an interview.
_____	_____	**4.** Anyone you know can be part of your job search network.
_____	_____	**5.** It doesn't matter if your skills don't match the job you want.
_____	_____	**6.** You shouldn't tell anybody you are job hunting.
_____	_____	**7.** Job hunting can take a lot of hard work.
_____	_____	**8.** State employment centers can help in your job search.

B. Revisit the Reading Strategy Pick any of the ideas below that were not part of the ideas you wrote on page 64. Discuss the ideas with a partner or small group.

- Your skills need to match the needs of the current job market.
- You can receive help to develop an education plan to brush up on your skills.
- Mention your skills when you are talking to employers.
- Let your friends and relatives know you are job hunting.

C. Think Beyond the Reading Think about this question and discuss it with a partner. Answer the question in writing if you wish.

What do you think are the three most important ideas to keep in mind while job hunting? Why?

Think About It: Identify the Main Idea

In any piece of writing, the **main idea** is the most important point a writer wants to make. A piece of writing can have several levels of main ideas.

- The whole piece of writing has one overall main idea.
- If the piece of writing has sections with subheads, each section has its own main idea.
- Within each section, each paragraph has its own main idea.

A. Look at Identifying the Main Idea

The outline below has the headings filled in for the first two sections of the article "Tips for Job Hunting." The main idea for the first section is also filled in. Reread the first section to see how the outline relates to the article.

Tips for Job Hunting

1. Know Your Skills and Abilities

   Section main idea: _Know what you are good at and what you enjoy doing._

2. Brush Up Your Skills

   Section main idea: _____

   _____

Now reread the second section, "Brush Up Your Skills," to see what its main idea might be. Write the main idea on the lines in the outline.

The main idea might be stated as "Identify necessary skills that need improvement and develop a plan to improve them."

B. Practice

The outline of the article is continued below. Reread each section of the article and then write a main idea statement. Notice that the third section, "Actively Search," is started for you. This section has four paragraphs. Each paragraph has a main idea. The main idea of the section and of the first paragraph are filled in to get you started.

---

3. Actively Search

Section main idea: ___<u>There are many ways to search for a job.</u>___

Paragraph 1 main idea: ___<u>Find out what jobs are available.</u>___

Paragraph 2 main idea: _____

_____

Paragraph 3 main idea: _____

_____

Paragraph 4 main idea: _____

_____

4. Knock on the Right Doors

Section main idea: _____

_____

5. Prepare for an Interview

Section main idea: _____

_____

▶ **Talk About It**

Imagine that you have an appointment for an interview with a company. Role-play the interview with a partner. Look at the list of Interview Tips on page 68 for help. Make up some information about the company first. One of you will play the role of interviewer. Then switch roles. Afterward, discuss what you would do differently next time.

Write About It: Write About an Interesting Job

Job hunting usually requires some research. You need to research the types of jobs that are available. You also need to research what skills and duties are required of a job you are interested in.

In this activity, you will research a job you're interested in. What kind of work is it? What hours and duties does it entail? What skills are needed? After you have researched the job, write about the information you found.

First, choose a job to research. Think of a job that sounds like a good match for you. Write the job title here:

_____

A. **Prewriting** In Lesson 2, you worked with a KWL chart. Because this writing requires some research, we will add *H,* **"H**ow I will find the information I want," to the chart. Copy the headings below on separate paper.

K	W	H	L
(What I already know about this job.)	(What I want to know about this job.)	(How I will find the information I want.)	(What I learned about this job.)

Before you begin your research, fill in the first three columns of the KWHL chart you made. Fill in *L,* "What I learned about this job," before you begin to write.

B. **Writing** Using your KWHL chart, write at least one paragraph describing your job choice. Include all of the information you feel is important. Be sure to include a main idea sentence in each paragraph.

▶ **Save your draft.** At the end of this unit, you will choose one of your drafts to work with further.

Life Skill: Fill In a Job Network Web

You can use a web to create your own job network. You know many people, probably more people than you think. They will have ideas about different jobs and companies. Many of these people can help you in your job search.

For example, look back at the web on page 67.

Notice that the person who drew that web can ask not only friends and relatives but also other people's friends and relatives for information about jobs.

Practice Make a web for yourself. Study the filled-in web for ideas. Before you make your own web, make lists to help you think of all the people you know. Your list might start with these categories:

- friends
- friends of friends
- family
- neighbors
- business acquaintances

- classmates
- people who work at school
- people who work at stores you visit
- people you see daily
- people you do business with

Now draw your own web on separate paper. Include everyone you can think of. Copy the model below to get started.

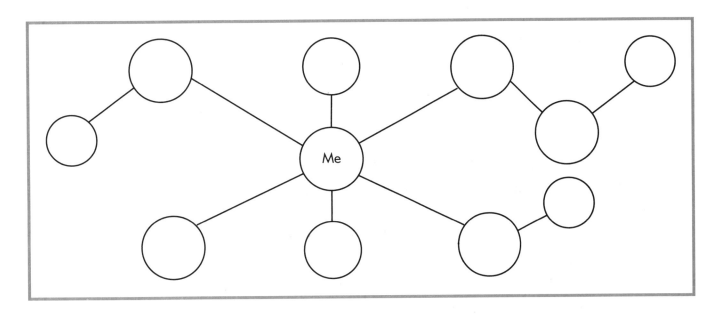

Writing Skills Mini-Lesson: Fixing Run-on Sentences

A **run-on sentence** is two or more independent clauses run together with no connecting word or punctuation. When you write complete, separate sentences, your ideas are easy to understand. If you run your sentences together without using connecting words, your ideas will not be clear. Run-on sentences are hard to read. Look at this example:

> I want a new job I need to make more money.

Here are three ways to fix run-on sentences like the one above.

1. Divide the run-on into separate sentences. Each sentence will have its own subject and verb, start with a capital letter, and end with a period.

   I want a new job. **I need** to make more money.

2. Use a comma and a connecting word like *and, but, or,* or *so* to join two independent clauses.

   I need to make more money, **so** I want a new job.

3. Use a connecting word like *when, after, because,* or *although* to create a dependent clause and join it to an independent clause. Remember to add a comma if the dependent clause comes first.

   - I want a new job **because** I need to make more money.
   - **Because** I need to make more money, I want a new job.

Practice On your own paper, fix these run-on sentences. Rewrite each one two ways.

1. The store needed a clerk I filled in an application.
2. The manager interviewed me I was a little nervous.
3. I liked the manager she seemed like a fair boss.
4. The interview ended the manager introduced me to the staff.
5. I got home the telephone rang.
6. The manager offered me the job I wanted to think about it first.
7. It was a good opportunity I decided to accept it.

Unit 2 Review

Reading Review

Kim Takes a Big Step

When Kim returned home with the application for the grocery store, she knew she needed help filling in the form. There were some terms she didn't understand. Kim was nervous about asking for help, but she was determined to fill the form in correctly. She wanted the job. She knew she would be a good cashier.

A friend recommended that Kim get help from the Department of Education and Training (D.E.T.). The next morning, Kim was at the door of the local D.E.T. office when it opened. Inez, a job specialist, could tell Kim was very nervous. She put Kim at ease. "Hundreds of people come in for just this kind of help," Inez told her.

Kim took the application out of her bag. Inez read through the entire form with her. Kim was both surprised and pleased that she could complete it with a little help. "Thank you," Kim said shyly. "It's important to me to fill this in well."

Kim hurried out of the D.E.T. office and took the bus to the grocery store. By 10:30 A.M. she had handed her application to the manager. The manager studied it carefully. Kim waited with her heart pounding. After a short time, he asked, "Could you come in tomorrow for an interview?"

"Oh, yes!" Kim replied happily. "I certainly can."

Choose the best answer to each question.

1. Kim was confident about
   (1) her ability to fill in an application
   (2) her ability to be a cashier
   (3) having a job interview
   (4) how to list her skills

2. Kim was afraid that if she didn't correctly fill in the job application,
   (1) she would have to take it back
   (2) she would not get the job
   (3) no one could help her
   (4) her friends would laugh at her

3. What was Kim determined to do?
   (1) find a job in a week
   (2) fill in the form without help
   (3) be a pharmacist
   (4) fill in the form correctly

4. What is this story mainly about?
   (1) what a job specialist does
   (2) how Kim found a job
   (3) how Kim applied for a job
   (4) what an interview is like

Writing Process

In Unit 2, you wrote three first drafts. Choose the piece that you would like to work with further. You will revise, edit, and make a final copy of this draft.

   _____ your description of your dream job (page 54)
   _____ your personal information sheet (page 62)
   _____ your description of an interesting job (page 72)

Find the first draft you chose. Then turn to page 160 in this book. Follow steps 3, 4, and 5 in the Writing Process to create a final draft.

As you revise, check your draft for this specific point:

Description of a dream job: Does the paragraph have a topic sentence that tells the main idea?

Personal information sheet: Is it filled in completely and correctly?

Description of an interesting job: Did you include all the information you felt was important?

Unit 3 A Sense of Community

What is a community? A community is a group of people who live in the same area and share the same neighborhood. But a community is more than just people who live near each other. A community is also a group of people who have some of the same goals and share some of the same problems. People in communities often work together to provide services for everyone to share. When neighborhoods have problems, people often learn to cooperate and work on solutions together. It is this "sense of community" that can make a neighborhood a real community.

▶ **Be an Active Reader**

As you read the selections in this unit
- Put a question mark (?) by things you do not understand.
- Underline words you do not know. Try to use context clues to figure them out.

After you read each selection in this unit
- Reread sections you marked with a question mark (?). If they still do not make sense, discuss them with a partner or your instructor.
- Look at words you underlined. Discuss any words you still don't understand with a partner or your instructor, or look them up in a dictionary.

Lesson 7

LEARNING GOALS

Strategy: Use your prior experience
Reading: Read an article
Skill: Recognize problems and solutions
Writing: Write about a problem and a solution
Life Skill: Use a phone book

Before You Read

Victoria Kearse wrote the article "Make Sure What You're Looking at Is Really What You See" while she was a student at The Learning Place in Syracuse, New York. In the article, Kearse gives suggestions on how her community can help teens stay out of trouble. Before you read her article, think back to your own **prior experiences,** experiences you have had in the past. What problems do you remember from your own teenage years?

What are your opinions on how to help teens in your community?
List some of them below.

_____

_____

_____

_____

_____

Preview the Reading

Preview the article by thinking about what the title might mean. Then read the first paragraph, and think about the title again. Based on that paragraph, what do you think the title refers to?

▶ **Use the Strategy**

As you read this article, think of your own experiences with teenagers. Compare them with the author's experience in her community. What are her concerns? Are they similar to yours?

Make Sure What You're Looking at Is Really What You See

Victoria Kearse

Living in the community, you see a lot of things going on. We tend to say there are dope pushers, just because we see a group of young men standing on the corner or hanging out in front of a store. How do you know all of them are selling drugs or are hoodlums? Do you know? Do you know for sure?

The reason why I said that is so you don't judge anyone just from looking at them or assuming you know. Now, yes, a lot of our kids sell drugs and do them, and steal and sell the item. That's so they can make money. We need to open the eyes of our community. Listen and see what needs to be done. Every adult in the community is a leader, whether you know it or not.

Yes, you are a leader. Some child somewhere is watching you and doing what you do and saying what you say. So we first must take a move to insure our children a safe and happy future. Talking loud and saying nothing is so easy to do. But speaking soft but firm to the ones who can make a change in our community is what needs to be done, to give our children a chance at life. We as being black know how hard it is for a black man to survive and to care for his family. That's why it is good to teach kids how to be a proper child at a young age and pray that it sticks with them.

When you were a teenager, how were you taught about proper behavior? According to the author, who should teach children today?

◀ Check-in

But we need something for them to do. The centers in our community are geared more toward the younger age groups. Some of our older children do go to some of the centers, but most of them don't. We need something like a sports-o-rama or a pool hall just for teens. Then we can have more to offer our teens and make new jobs, too. It's also a way to put money back into the community. I know it wouldn't stop all the crime in the community, but it would help.

Let's pull together as one and do what needs to be done about this problem. Because our children are our today and tomorrow, and we cannot afford to lose them.

▶ **Final Check-in**

Think of your own teenage experience. Is it important to have activities and centers strictly for teens? Why or why not?

Do Teenagers Need Help?

Victoria Kearse's article focuses on the needs of teenagers in her community. She maintains that teenagers need adult leadership and good role models to keep them from committing crimes. She also believes that teens need community recreation centers to provide them with places to gather and have fun. Do you agree with her?

Below is a bar graph that shows the number of juvenile[1] inmates in U.S. prisons for the years 1988 through 1993.

To read the graph, look at a date at the bottom, such as 1988. Find the number along the left side of the graph that most closely aligns with the bar for 1988. This bar is more than halfway between 1,500 and 1,750. You can estimate that there were close to 1,700 juveniles in U.S. prisons in 1988.

Answer the questions below about the graph.

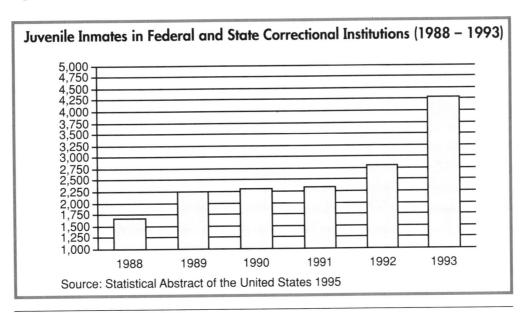

Juvenile Inmates in Federal and State Correctional Institutions (1988 – 1993)

Source: Statistical Abstract of the United States 1995

1. **juvenile:** a young person.

- About how many juveniles were in prisons in 1989? _____

- About how many juveniles were in prisons in 1992? _____

- What year shows the greatest increase in juvenile inmates? _____

You probably answered that there were about 2,250 juveniles in prison in 1989 and about 2,800 in 1992. The greatest increase in juvenile inmates happened in 1993.

After You Read

A. **Comprehension Check** Check **True** if the statement reflects the author's opinion or the information in the graph. Check **False** if it does not.

True	False	
_____	_____	1. Don't judge people just by looking at them.
_____	_____	2. Few adults can be leaders.
_____	_____	3. Teens need their own centers.
_____	_____	4. Teen centers benefit only teens.
_____	_____	5. Children do what they see adults do.
_____	_____	6. There are no community centers for young children.
_____	_____	7. There were more teenagers in prison in 1988 than in 1990.
_____	_____	8. The number of teenagers in prison increased each year between 1988 and 1993.

B. **Revisit the Reading Strategy** Think of your own experiences with teenagers. Check **Yes** or **No** to show whether your experiences are like those of the author. Then discuss your responses with a partner or small group.

Yes	No	
_____	_____	1. Teenagers are mainly regarded with suspicion.
_____	_____	2. Adults are authority figures for most teenagers.
_____	_____	3. Teenage crime is a major issue.
_____	_____	4. Your community has centers for young children.
_____	_____	5. Your community provides a teen center.

C. **Think Beyond the Reading** Think about these questions and discuss them with a partner. Answer the questions in writing if you wish.

1. Do the teenagers you know feel they are a part of a community, or do they feel isolated from both adults and younger children? If so, how can they become more involved?

2. Can teenagers help build a better environment for themselves? For example, how could they help raise money to build a teen center?

Think About It: Recognize Problems and Solutions

You learned about recognizing **problems** and **solutions** in Lesson 1.
To solve a problem, you need to take certain steps.

> **Problem-Solving Process**
>
> **Step 1.** Identify the problem.
> **Step 2.** Identify its cause or causes.
> **Step 3.** Think of several possible solutions.
> **Step 4.** Evaluate the possible solutions and choose the best one.
> **Step 5.** Develop a plan to carry out the solution, and implement it.

A. Look at Problems and Solutions

In the excerpt below, the author follows Step 1, identifying
a community-wide problem:

> ▶ Now, yes, a lot of our kids sell drugs and do them, and steal
> and sell the item.

Next the author follows Step 2 and identifies one of the causes:

> ▶ That's so they can make money.

Then the author goes on to Step 3, suggesting possible solutions:

> ▶ We need to open the eyes of our community. Listen and see
> what needs to be done.

Step 1: What is the problem? _____

Step 2: What cause is identified? _____

Step 3: What solution is suggested? _____

The author says the problem is that teenagers sell drugs and steal. They do it
to get money. She suggests that the community pay attention to teenagers'
needs.

B. Practice Read the excerpt below. Then fill in the problem and solution worksheet that follows.

▶ But we need something for them to do. The centers in our community are geared more toward the younger age groups. Some of our older children do go to some of the centers, but most of them don't. We need something like a sports-o-rama or a pool hall just for teens. . . . I know it wouldn't stop all the crime in the community, but it would help. Let's pull together as one and do what needs to be done about this problem.

Problem/Solution Worksheet

Step 1. What is the problem?

_____

Step 2. What causes are identified?

_____

_____

Step 3. What possible solutions does the author give?

_____

_____

_____

_____

▶ **Talk About It**

With a partner or small group, discuss the problems and solutions highlighted in Victoria Kearse's article. Does your community experience similar problems? What has the community done about its problems? What could it do? Are Kearse's suggested solutions good ones? Why or why not?

Write About It: Write About a Problem and a Solution

In any community there are many problems that need to be solved. Explore one of your community's problems and suggest solutions. Choose one of these topics, or one of your own.

- teenagers using drugs
- not enough activities for teenagers
- lack of people to work with teenagers

- not enough jobs
- high housing costs
- no inexpensive entertainment

A. Prewriting Fill out this worksheet with your thoughts on your topic.

Problem/Solution Worksheet

1. What is the problem? _____

2. What causes the problem? _____

3. What are some possible solutions? _____

_____

_____

_____

4. What is the best solution? Why is it the best?

_____

_____

_____

B. Writing Write three paragraphs about the problem and the possible solutions. Use the ideas you included in the worksheet above. In the first paragraph, describe the problem and its causes. In the second paragraph, describe possible solutions. In the third paragraph, explain the best solution and why it is the best.

▶ **Save your draft.** At the end of this unit, you will choose one of your drafts to work with further.

Life Skill: Use a Phone Book

Most communities have resources to help people solve problems. You can use your phone book to find out what resources are available in your community.

You can find out about services by calling community and government agencies, which are listed in the blue pages of many phone books. Or look for a list of community services in the phone book's table of contents.

Try finding some specific information in this phone book sample:

```
Elderly Services—See SENIOR CITIZENS SERVICES
Employment Services—See LABOR DEPARTMENT
Fire
        Emergency..................................................911
        Non–Emergency..............................555-6666
Food  Complaints....................................555-7480
Food Stamp Hotline
        Toll  Free....................................800-555-8636
Garbage & Trash Collection.....................555-5000
```

1. What phone number would you dial to find out what day garbage is

    picked up on your block? _____

2. What words would you look up to find out about services for older people?

    _____

3. What number would you dial to report a fire? _____

    Now look in your phone book to find phone numbers for the following
    community and government services. Write a phone number for each.
    Your phone book may have different names for some listings.

    County Clerk _____   Parks and Recreation _____

    Employment Assistance _____   Poison Control Center _____

    Health Clinic _____   Public Libraries _____

    Legal Assistance _____   Voter Registration _____

Practice Practice using the phone book to find community resources that can help you with a problem. For example, maybe you want to find a day-care center for your child. Or you may need to locate a government program to help an elderly relative maintain her home.

Think of a community resource you want to find to help you solve a problem. Complete each step below.

1. Define what your problem is or what you need.

_____

2. Decide what type of resource might help you.

_____

3. Think of some questions you need to ask.

_____

_____

_____

4. Pick two possible resources from the phone book. List them here with their phone numbers.

Resource name	Phone number

5. Call each service to get answers to the questions you wrote. Fill in the answers you receive on the lines below.

Name _____

Answers to your questions _____

_____

Name _____

Answers to your questions _____

_____

Lesson 8

LEARNING GOALS

Strategy: Predict features
Reading: Read an introduction, a map, and a key
Skill: Follow directions
Writing: Write directions
Life Skill: Draw a map

Before You Read

In this lesson you will read about Juan, a father who decides to take his children to a large park in their community to play. Then you will follow their trip through the park on a map.

What kinds of things do you think they will find in the park? **Predict features** of the park. In other words, figure out in advance what things might be in the park. Think about a park you have been in. List some things park visitors might see.

_____

_____

_____

_____

_____

Preview the Reading

Look at the picture. Read the title and the first two sentences of the reading. These give hints that Juan is going to take his boys to a park. Now preview the map and the first few items in the key to get an idea of what they can find in this park.

▶ **Use the Strategy**

Find some features you might want to see in the park by looking at the map and reading the key.

Let's Go Out!

It's a warm, sunny day. Juan's two young boys beg their dad to take them to a park. Their small apartment has no yard. Carlos and Ramon want to play outside. Juan decides to take them to Boston Common,[1] a famous park in Boston.

This week, Juan watched a TV program about Boston Common. He learned that it is America's oldest park. People have come to the Common for over 360 years. Juan also learned that the park has many places for kids to explore.

Boston Common looks like a perfect place to take two lively boys. It has many open spaces without "Keep Off" signs.

Juan will need to use the map on page 90 to find the attractions in the park. Notice that there are numbers at various places on the map. The key next to the map tells which attraction each number stands for. Read the key and find each attraction on the map.

---

1. common: a public area open to the community.

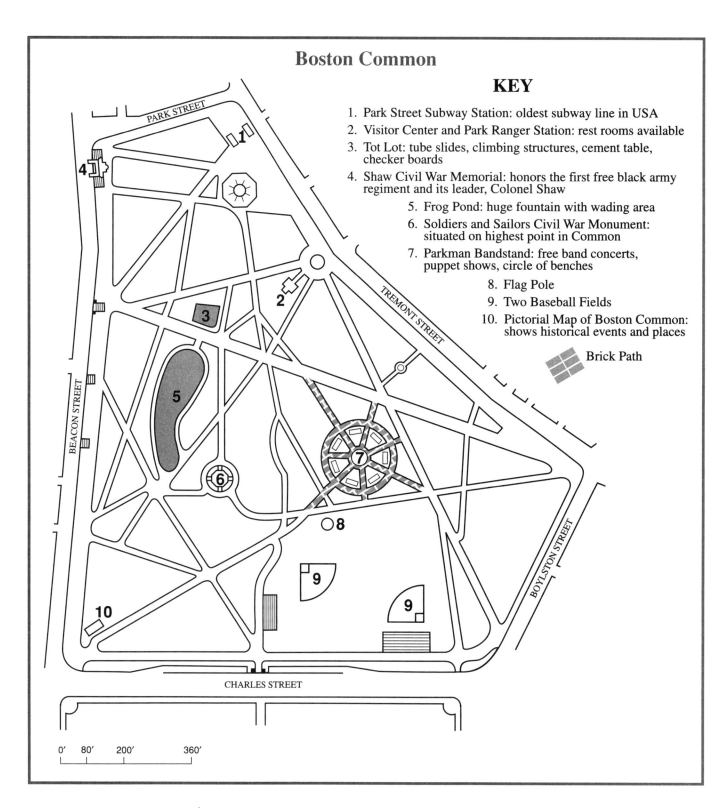

Boston Common

KEY

1. Park Street Subway Station: oldest subway line in USA
2. Visitor Center and Park Ranger Station: rest rooms available
3. Tot Lot: tube slides, climbing structures, cement table, checker boards
4. Shaw Civil War Memorial: honors the first free black army regiment and its leader, Colonel Shaw
5. Frog Pond: huge fountain with wading area
6. Soldiers and Sailors Civil War Monument: situated on highest point in Common
7. Parkman Bandstand: free band concerts, puppet shows, circle of benches
8. Flag Pole
9. Two Baseball Fields
10. Pictorial Map of Boston Common: shows historical events and places

⊞⊞ Brick Path

PARK STREET

TREMONT STREET

BEACON STREET

BOYLSTON STREET

CHARLES STREET

0'   80'   200'   360'

▶ **Check-in**

Have you found all 10 places on the map? If not, review them with a partner or an instructor.

After You Read

A. Comprehension Check

1. Check whether each statement is **True** or **False.**

True	False	
_____	_____	**a.** Carlos and Ramon wanted to go to the park because it is a famous place.
_____	_____	**b.** The Tot Lot is at the edge of the park, by the street.
_____	_____	**c.** Juan's boys could go wading at the Frog Pond.
_____	_____	**d.** You could identify places on this map without using the key.
_____	_____	**e.** Juan heard about Boston Common on TV.
_____	_____	**f.** The park has only one baseball field.
_____	_____	**g.** Boston Common is the oldest park in the U.S.
_____	_____	**h.** There are two Civil War monuments in the park.

2. Where would you find rest rooms? Write the number from the key. _____

3. Where would people go to play softball? _____

4. Where would you find another map of the Common? _____

B. Revisit the Reading Strategy
Look back at the predictions you made on page 88 telling what features might be found on Boston Common. Did your predictions match what you found on the map? Do you think Boston Common is different from other parks you have been to? In what ways?

C. Think Beyond the Reading
Think about these questions and discuss them with a partner. Answer the questions in writing if you wish.

1. How do parks improve life for the people in a community? Can parks also have negative effects on the community? What are they?

2. What features would you build into a park you were planning for your community? Why would you include each feature? Who would most likely benefit from each one?

Think About It: Follow Directions

Directions are usually given as a series of steps. To follow directions, you do what each step tells you to do. For example, you are following directions when someone tells you how to drive to their house, and you turn onto each street they tell you to take. Pay attention to clue words: *next, before, after,* and *soon* tell when to do something; words like *left, right, straight ahead,* and *follow the diagonal* tell where you should go. Notice the clue words underlined in the directions below:

- To find Room 152, <u>first</u> enter the building by the <u>left side</u> door.
- Go <u>straight ahead</u> down the narrow hallway.
- <u>After</u> the water cooler, <u>turn right</u>.
- Room 152 is <u>at the end</u> of the hallway <u>on the left</u>.

A. Look at Following Directions

When you have to follow directions to go someplace, you can often look at a map to see the exact route. On the map of Boston Common, you must use the map key to identify the names of places labeled by numbers on the map. For example, in the park, Juan first went to number 2 on the map. Look at the key. Where did he go?

_____

He went to the Visitor Center and Park Ranger Station.

Practice following a set of directions using the Boston Common map. Follow the directions below. See where you end up.

1. Start at the Charles Street entrance in the middle of the block. The baseball fields will be on the right.
2. Take the diagonal path that bears left into the park.
3. The path will cross another path. Keep walking straight ahead until you come to the next intersection. Take a sharp right.
4. Walk a short way until you come to the highest point in the Common. Where are you?

_____

You should be at the Soldiers and Sailors Civil War Monument.

B. Practice The following sets of directions are mystery walks. Follow the steps on the map of the Boston Common to find out where you end up in the park.

1. The first mystery walk goes to a favorite spot for children.
   - Start at number 4, the Shaw Civil War Memorial. Walk along the path that borders Beacon Street.
   - When you come to the place where three paths go into the park, take the path on your right.
   - Proceed straight through the first intersection to the next intersection.
   - Turn left. Your destination will be on your left.

   Where did you end up? _____

2. The second mystery walk goes to a good place for a concert.
   - Enter the park at the corner of Tremont and Boylston Streets.
   - Follow the wide path toward the center of the park.
   - After the second intersection, turn left onto a brick path.
   - Follow the brick path for a short distance, through the circle of benches.

   Where did you end up? _____

 Talk About It

Many of us have been stopped by someone who wants directions. Giving clear directions is an important skill. You should include all the significant points, and leave out confusing details. Give a partner directions to a place that he or she has not been to. Then, reverse roles. See if you can repeat each other's directions. If so, they are probably clear.

Write About It: Write Directions

If someone is going to visit your home for the first time, you may want to give them written directions. In this activity you will write directions to your home.

A. Prewriting Decide where your visitor will be coming from, so you know where your directions should begin. It may help to look at a street map of your community.

B. Writing Now write the directions to your home. Follow these tips.

Tips for Writing Directions

- Begin at the spot where your guest will start, or begin at a well-known starting point, such as a major highway or a familiar landmark in your community.
- Be clear whether the directions are for travel by bus, car, or foot.
- Include distances, such as 2 miles, 3 blocks, and so on.
- Include any turns your guest will have to make. Give street names or route numbers for all turns.
- Mention any prominent landmarks your guest will pass.

Write each direction as a separate step. Number each step in your directions. Write a rough draft here. Include as few or as many steps as needed.

_____

_____

_____

_____

_____

_____

▶ **Save your draft.** At the end of this unit, you will choose one of your drafts to work with further.

Life Skill: Draw a Map

It is often said that a picture is worth a thousand words. To make the written instructions to your home even clearer, you can draw a pictorial map to go along with them.

The sample map on this page gives directions by car or by foot to a person's home. The shaded line leads from the bus station to the home. Follow the shaded line to see what landmarks are included to help the map user. What street do you follow from the bus station? Do you turn before or after crossing railroad tracks?

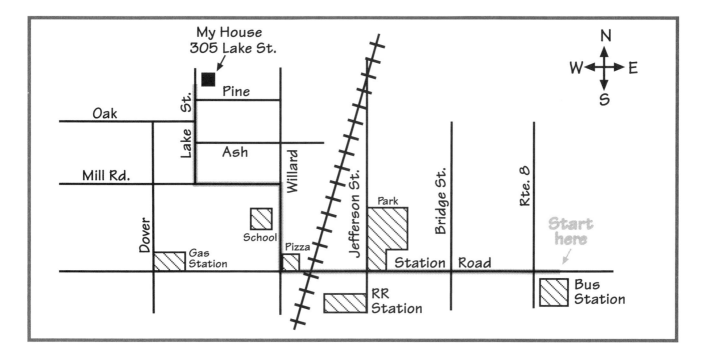

If you said "Station Road" and "after," you are following the sample map correctly.

Practice Now draw a map to your own home on a separate piece of paper. Your map needs to show in picture form all the information that you wrote in the activity on page 94. Be sure to label all important landmarks and street names. Do not include unnecessary or confusing information. Clearly label the starting point and end point of your directions.

After you have completed your map, trade maps with a partner. See if you understand how to follow each other's maps.

Lesson 9

LEARNING GOALS

Strategy: Predict content
Reading: Read a brochure
Skill: Locate key facts
Writing: Write an announcement
Life Skill: Use the library as a community resource

Before You Read

You probably know where to find at least one public library in your community. Do you know how many different materials and services are provided by libraries? The brochure "Your Library: A Major Community Resource" tells about the services of one community library. There are many public libraries like it.

You can probably **predict** some of the **content** of a brochure that describes the materials and services found in a library. Check the services and materials you think you would find listed in a brochure about a typical library.

_____	videotapes to borrow	_____	grocery store coupons
_____	daily newspapers	_____	English classes
_____	live music programs	_____	audiocassettes to borrow
_____	job hunting resources	_____	movies to borrow
_____	reference materials	_____	local art exhibits
_____	programs for children	_____	apartment rental information

Preview the Reading

Preview the brochure by looking at the headings in the text. Did you know that libraries provide many of these services? Do any headings describe services that you wouldn't have predicted?

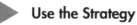 **Use the Strategy**

Read each heading and predict one thing that the text will include. As you read, note how many of your predictions are actually mentioned in the text.

Your Library: A Major Community Resource

Welcome to your public library. Books and magazines are just part of the many services at the library. This library has services and activities for everyone. Most of our services are free.

Library Materials to Check Out

We have books for people of all ages, magazines, pamphlets, and large-print books. You can also borrow tapes of movies and music, audiotapes of books, and passes to local museums.

Materials for Use in the Library

New issues of magazines, reference books, computers, Internet connections and daily papers are available for use in the library. Past issues of *The New York Times* can be viewed on microfilm.

840 Maple Street, Centerville • Phone: 555-2121
Library Hours
Monday-Thursday 9-8   Friday and Saturday 9-5
Sunday (September-May) 1-5

Library Services

Computer Catalog

The library has a Library Network Computer Catalog to search for specific titles, subjects, or authors. It is located on the first floor, Room 100, and is available during regular library hours. A one-session class on how to use the Computer Catalog is offered once a month. Dates and times are listed in Room 100.

Inter-Library Loan

Do you need a book or magazine that is not in this library or that is out on loan? We can request it for you from another library. This library is joined with 20 other libraries through a library network.

Home Delivery Service

Are you unable to come to the library because of illness or a disability? You are eligible for monthly delivery of circulating books and magazines. This includes audio books and large-print books.

Museum Passes

You may borrow a free pass for museum admissions. Inquire at the reference desk.

Job Hunting

The library can help you search for a job. Inquire about job resources at the reference desk.

English for ESL Students

For library users whose first language is not English, the library has materials that teach English as a Second Language (ESL). There are books, videos and audiocassettes that can be used in the library or checked out. Individual study rooms are available for use.

How many of your predictions have been mentioned so far?

◀ Check-in

Library Activities

Friday Night at the Movies

Award-winning movies every Friday at 8:00 P.M. Refreshments courtesy of the Library Association.

Wednesday Morning Slide Shows

Area residents share exciting adventures from their travels around the world.

A few samples from the past: Tracking Wild Animals in Africa, Hiking the Alaskan Wilderness, and Revisiting Vietnam. Check with the library for dates and times.

Jazz on Tape

Tenth year for this well-attended program. September-June, Wednesday evenings at 7:30 P.M.

You name it—they play it. Call for exact program.

Art Exhibits

Exhibits feature works by community members from many cultures.

Watch for announcements of opening receptions.

Children's Programs

Special Events for Children

Events include magic shows, music programs, storytellers, and talks by favorite authors. Additional programs during school vacations. Monthly program guides available.

Toddler Program

Stories and activities feature puppets, music, and movement. September-June, Tuesdays 10:00-11:00 A.M.

School-age Program

Crafts projects use the themes of books children love. September-May, third Thursday of the month 4:00-5:30 P.M.

▶ **Final Check-in**

Did the headings help you correctly predict the information contained in the brochure? Did you also read information you didn't predict?

Join Us for a Community Folk Sing

Featuring: Local folk singer, Andy Wilkins
When: July 10 at 7:00 P.M.
Where: Centerville Library Courtyard

Andy Wilkins will play his guitar and mandolin.
You can learn new songs and request old favorites.

Refreshments provided during intermission.

Sponsored by Friends of the Library
Rain date: July 12 at 7:00 P.M.

New! Check It Out!

Two free family passes to the Science Museum
now available through the Centerville Library

- Borrowers must have a current library card.
- Each pass will admit up to four people.
- Children under 16 must be accompanied by an adult.

- Passes must be reserved in advance.
- Reserve in person or by phone.
- State what day you want to visit the museum.
- A pass can be used only on that day.
- Return pass the following day.

Call the library for more information: 555-2121
Inquire about other museum passes that are available.

After You Read

A. Comprehension Check

1. Which two materials can be checked out of the library?
   (1) large-print books and reference books
   (2) computers and older magazines
   (3) children's books and audiotapes
   (4) CDs and current magazines

2. The Library Network Computer Catalog
   (1) lists only authors of books
   (2) lists subjects, authors, and titles
   (3) is used only by librarians
   (4) is not free

3. How can you learn to use the Library Network Computer Catalog?
   (1) go to night school
   (2) read a book on it
   (3) attend a one-session class
   (4) use a computer at home

4. The children's programs
   (1) feature a variety of events
   (2) close down during school vacations
   (3) are only for school-age children
   (4) are mainly story hours

B. Revisit the Reading Strategy
Look at the materials and services you checked on page 96. Do your predictions match what you found in the brochure? Did your predictions help you focus on the facts in the brochure?

C. Think Beyond the Reading
Think about these questions and discuss them with a partner. Answer the questions in writing if you wish.

People receive news and information from many sources: television, radio, newspapers, magazines, books, and computers. What sources do you use most to get news and information? Have these sources changed in the last 10 years? What sources do you think you will be using most 10 years from now?

Think About It: Locate Key Facts

When you read informative material, be sure to look for the **key facts.**
These are facts that give you essential information about the topic. Often,
the key facts are answers to *who, what, where, when, why,* and *how* questions.

A. Look at Locating Key Facts

Informational materials such as library brochures or pamphlets contain
many key facts. Read the following information about a class on using the
library's computer catalog. Find the key facts that tell *what dates the class
is offered* and *where to sign up for the class.* Underline these facts.

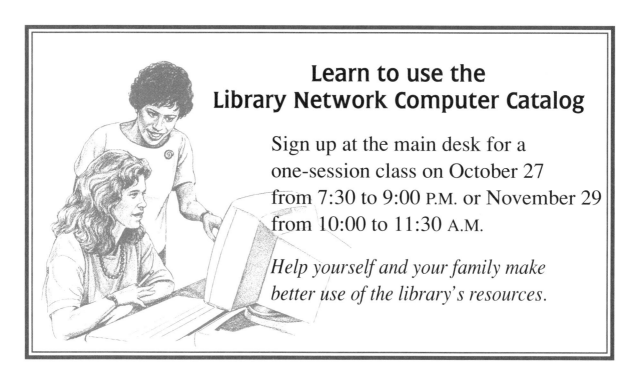

**Learn to use the
Library Network Computer Catalog**

Sign up at the main desk for a
one-session class on October 27
from 7:30 to 9:00 P.M. or November 29
from 10:00 to 11:30 A.M.

*Help yourself and your family make
better use of the library's resources.*

Did you underline "October 27," "November 29," and "main desk"? If so,
you found the facts you were looking for.

B. Practice Read the announcements and locate the key facts. Write them on the lines.

Join Us for a Community Folk Sing

Featuring: Local folk singer, Andy Wilkins
When: July 10 at 7:00 P.M.
Where: Centerville Library Courtyard

Andy Wilkins will play his guitar and mandolin. You can learn new songs and request old favorites.

Refreshments provided during intermission.

Sponsored by Friends of the Library
Rain date: July 12 at 7:00 P.M.

---

1. What? _____   Who? _____

When? _____   Where? _____

Computer Catalog
The library has a Library Network Computer Catalog to search for specific titles, subjects, or authors. It is located on the first floor, Room 100, and is available during regular library hours. A one-session class on how to use the Computer Catalog is offered once a month. Dates and times are listed in Room 100.

2. What? _____

Why? _____

Where? _____

When? _____

▶ **Talk About It**
Think of a question the library can answer for you. First role-play with a partner. Be sure to tell the key facts of your question, such as why you are calling and what you want to know. Then actually make the phone call and share the information with the group.

Write About It: Write an Announcement

Many libraries have a community bulletin board on which you can post announcements. In this activity, you will write an announcement to post on a community bulletin board. For example, you might advertise a school bake sale or something you want to sell or buy. You may have lost something near the library, or you may have a room for rent.

A. Prewriting Think about what you will write in your announcement. List the key facts below.

1. What? _____

2. Who? _____

3. When? _____

4. Where? _____

5. Why? _____

6. Other details (such as cost) _____

_____

B. Writing After you have listed your key facts, write a first draft of your announcement on separate paper. Be sure your announcement includes all the key facts you listed.

Get ideas about how to format your announcement by looking at the announcements on page 100, or look at announcements on bulletin boards.

Here are some tips:
- Key words should be in bold or larger letters.
- Present some information in list form, so it is easy to read.
- Make sure the words are large enough to be easily read.
- Put phone numbers and addresses at the top or bottom, so they are easy to find.

▶ **Save your draft.** At the end of this unit, you will choose one of your drafts to work with further.

Life Skill: Use the Library as a Community Resource

Your public library is a valuable community resource. You can find a variety of services at the library. Your own library card is your key to many of these free services.

The Library Card

It is very simple to apply for a library card. When you apply, bring something with you that shows your name and address, such as your driver's license or your voter registration card. In most communities, children age 5 and over can also get library cards with a parent's approval.

Practice Fill out this sample library card application.

No. _____

Do not write above this line.

I apply for the right to use the library and agree to comply with all its rules and regulations, as well as to give immediate notice of any change of address.

Date: _____

First and Last Name: _____

Street Address: _____

City, State: _____ ZIP: _____

Telephone: (home)_____ (work)_____

▶ Writing Skills Mini-Lesson: Correcting Usage Problems

When you write, watch out for these common usage problems.

1. **Do not use a double negative.** Use only one negative word or word part *(no, not, n't, none)* in a sentence to express a negative idea.
   > **Wrong:** The teenagers did**n't** have **nothing** to do.
   > **Right:** The teenagers did**n't** have **anything** to do.
   > **Right:** The teenagers had **nothing** to do.

2. **Do not use double comparisons.** To show comparisons, add the suffixes *-er* or *-est* to most one-syllable words. Use the words *more* and *most* with longer words. Do not use both forms together.
   > **Wrong:** They were **more** bigg**er**/the **most** bigg**est**.
   > **Right:** They were bigg**er**/the bigg**est**.

3. **Use the word *good* to describe a person, place, or thing. Use the word *well* to describe an action.** *Good* tells what someone or something is like. *Well* tells how something is done.
   > **Wrong:** They play **good**. They are **well** players.
   > **Right:** They play **well**. They are **good** players.

Practice Underline the errors in the paragraph below. On your own paper, copy the paragraph, making all necessary corrections.

The teenagers in my neighborhood didn't have nothing to do, and

they didn't have nowhere to go. They made noise and littered, but the

most biggest problem was the fear they caused in the community. Some

of the more older people were afraid to go out. Finally, we held a

community meeting and decided to start a sports program. Now the

program is running good, and we don't have no more problems.

Unit 3 Review

Reading Review

Where Is Ramon?

Juan's boys, Carlos and Ramon, had a great time in the Boston Common. First they ran up and down some of the walkways. Then 6-year-old Carlos started to roll down the big hill. Ramon followed right after him. When they grew tired of rolling, Juan took them to the Tot Lot. At first the boys hung back and watched other kids go down the tube slides. Finally, they joined in.

While the boys played, Juan looked through a newspaper. An insert about an upcoming Puerto Rican festival caught his eye. Juan glanced at the pictures. They reminded him of his childhood.

Suddenly, Juan felt a tug on his sleeve. Carlos was peering up at him with a worried look on his face. "Dad, Ramon's gone. I don't know where he is." Carlos started to cry. He was worried about his younger brother.

Juan jumped up. He ran to other parents, asking, "Have you seen my son? He's four. He's wearing blue jeans and a plaid shirt." Everyone said no. But then one woman said she had seen a boy dressed that way chasing after a teenage girl with a puppy. The teenager was heading up the hill. The woman thought the boy and girl were together.

Juan knew how badly Ramon wanted a dog. He thought the boy was probably his son. Juan could not believe how fast Ramon had disappeared. He felt it had been just a few seconds since he last saw him sliding down a tube slide.

Juan and Carlos raced up the hill. They got to the top and looked around in all directions. Ramon was not in sight. Just then, Juan heard a dog yapping on the other side of a monument.

Juan rushed to the back of the monument. There was Ramon—all smiles—with a furry collie puppy in his lap.

Choose the best answer to each question.

1. What was Juan's main problem in the story?
   (1) His son doesn't have a dog.
   (2) His younger son is missing.
   (3) He misses his childhood.
   (4) He can't find the bandstand.

2. What did Juan do first to solve his problem?
   (1) He looked for a park ranger.
   (2) He jumped up and asked people if they had seen Ramon.
   (3) He rushed out of the Tot Lot.
   (4) He asked Carlos to go look for Ramon in the Tot Lot.

3. What was the clue that led to the solution to Juan's problem?
   (1) Juan's quick action
   (2) the teenage girl's actions
   (3) information from other children
   (4) the sound of a yapping puppy

Writing Process

In Unit 3, you wrote three first drafts. Choose the piece that you would like to work with further. You will revise, edit, and make a final copy of this draft.

_____ your problem and solution paragraphs (page 85)
_____ the directions to your home (page 94)
_____ your announcement for a bulletin board (page 104)

Find the first draft you chose. Then turn to page 160 in this book. Follow steps 3, 4, and 5 in the Writing Process to create a final draft.

As you revise, check your draft for this specific point:
Paragraphs: Did you state the problem and solution specifically?
Directions: Did you include all turns?
Announcement: Did you include all essential facts about the topic?

Unit 4 Crime and the Law

Crime and the law: One tears society apart and the other tries to hold it together. Crime and the law affect all our lives, even if we have never had a personal experience with either. Laws are made to protect the rights of individuals and society in general. When crime threatens our security, we want the laws enforced. In this unit, you will read about some famous legal cases that went all the way to the Supreme Court before they became the law of the land. You will also read some views on neighborhood violence. Finally, you will read an amusing account of how a robbery was foiled.

▶ **Be an Active Reader**

As you read the selections in this unit
- Put a question mark (?) by things you do not understand.
- Underline words you do not know. Try to use context clues to figure them out.

After you read each selection in this unit
- Reread sections you marked with a question mark (?). If they still do not make sense, discuss them with a partner or your instructor.
- Look at words you underlined. Discuss any words you still don't understand with a partner or your instructor, or look them up in a dictionary.

Lesson 10 ▶ LEARNING GOALS

Strategy: Use your prior knowledge
Reading: Read an article
Skill: Apply information
Writing: Write your opinion
Life Skill: Read a line graph

Before You Read

In this lesson, you will read brief accounts of three famous Supreme Court cases. These cases continue to have an influence on the lives of many people.

Use your **prior knowledge,** information you already know, to see if you can explain some of the ideas that became famous during these court cases.

1. In the 1950s, some states had *segregated* public schools. Based on what you already know, explain what a segregated school was. _____

   _____

   _____

2. What do you think it means to be *assured legal help* if you are accused of a crime? _____

   _____

   _____

Preview the Reading

To preview the article, read the first two paragraphs in each of the three sections. Predict what might make each situation turn into a case for the Supreme Court.

Three "Little" People Who Changed U.S. History

from *Scholastic Update*

> "WE CONCLUDE THAT IN THE FIELD OF PUBLIC EDUCATION THE DOCTRINE[1] OF 'SEPARATE BUT EQUAL' HAS NO PLACE. SEPARATE EDUCATIONAL FACILITIES ARE INHERENTLY[2] UNEQUAL."
>
> *Oliver L. Brown, et al. v. Board of Education of Topeka, Kansas,* United States Supreme Court, May 17, 1954.

Brown v. Board of Education, 1954

Linda Brown lived four blocks from Sumner Elementary School in Topeka, Kansas. But she couldn't go there. Sumner accepted only white students. Linda was black.

Linda's father, Oliver, was tired of having to watch his daughter walk six blocks every day, wait for a bus, and head off to a black school three miles away. So when she was 7, he tried to enroll her in Sumner.

Kansas was one of 18 states in 1951 where segregation was legal. Linda was quickly rejected. But with the help of a lawyer named Thurgood Marshall, Oliver Brown sued the Board of Education of Topeka. He sued for an end to segregated schools.

---

1. doctrine: a principle of law.
2. inherently: naturally, essentially.

Three years later, the Supreme Court voted 9–0 in favor of Brown. It was a major victory for the civil rights movement. The Court agreed that forced segregation "generates a feeling of inferiority" among minorities. It rejected the concept of "separate but equal" facilities—a rule that had stood since 1892.

But segregation did not die easily. Many states refused to adhere to[3] the Court's ruling. It took years of protest by concerned citizens before states such as Alabama, Mississippi, and Louisiana allowed blacks and whites to sit together in the same classrooms.

Thurgood Marshall later became a justice of the Supreme Court. And Linda Brown, now Linda Brown Smith, is a grandmother.

She still lives in Topeka, where she teaches piano. But her important place in American history has not brought her happiness. In 1986, Smith told *People* magazine, "I am real bitter." Despite the end to legal segregation, Topeka's elementary schools are still "segregated." Blacks and whites live in separate neighborhoods and go to separate schools. "My children weren't . . . exposed to all races in school, and that is a big part of growing up and preparing for adulthood." She does not want the same fate for her grandchildren. She has called on the local school board to further integrate Topeka's schools.

Ironically,[4] after fighting to get into the school closest to her neighborhood, Smith now favors busing children to different schools to promote racial diversity.

◀ Check-in

Gideon v. Wainwright, 1963

Clarence Gideon had been in and out of prison for much of his 51 years, usually on charges of petty thievery. So it was no surprise when, in 1961, police picked him up for breaking and entering a pool hall in Panama City, Florida.

What did you remember about this famous case? Before you read this article, did you know that schools had once been segregated? Why did people work so hard to change segregated schools?

---

3. adhere to: be true to, follow.
4. ironically: opposite of what you might expect.

The U.S. Supreme Court in 1965. Left to right, standing: Associate justices Byron R. White; William J. Brennan Jr.; Potter Stewart; and Abe Fortas. Seated: Tom C. Clark; Hugo L. Black; Chief Justice Earl Warren; William O. Douglas; and John M. Harlan.

But Gideon said he was innocent. He was too poor to afford a lawyer. He demanded the court appoint him one.

Under Florida law, only accused murderers were given court-appointed lawyers. Gideon was forced to represent himself. He was convicted. He was sentenced to five years in jail.

From his cell in the Florida State penitentiary, Gideon, prisoner #003826, began studying the law. His reading convinced him that he had been denied his right to legal representation.

In 1962, Gideon sent a package to the Supreme Court. The letter inside was handwritten in pencil. Using the legal terms he had learned, Gideon asked the Court to overturn his conviction. By denying him a lawyer, he said, the Florida court had denied him his right to "due process of law."

The Court agreed to hear Gideon's case. It was filed against Louis L. Wainwright, the director of Florida prisons.

The panel voted 9–0 in favor of Gideon. "It is intolerable[5] in a nation which proclaims equal justice under the law . . . that anyone should be handicapped in defending himself simply because he happens to be poor," the Court said. From then on, all people accused of crimes were entitled to legal representation.

---

5. **intolerable:** unbearable, outrageous.

Gideon received a new trial. A lawyer from the American Civil Liberties Union offered to represent him. But ironically, after fighting so hard for the right to legal representation, Gideon fired the lawyer on his first day back in court. He said he would rather represent himself.

But this time, the judge refused to allow Gideon to represent himself. The court appointed Gideon a lawyer of his choosing. The new lawyer won Gideon an acquittal.[6] That night, the newly free man went to the pool hall for a visit.

Before he died in 1972, a reporter asked him, "Do you feel like you accomplished something?"

Gideon replied, "Well, I did."

◀ Check-in

Miranda v. Arizona, 1966

Ernesto Miranda was working in a Phoenix warehouse when the Arizona police arrested him. He was charged with kidnapping and rape. After hours of questioning, Miranda confessed to the crimes. In 1963, he was sentenced to 20–30 years in prison.

But his lawyer appealed the judgment. He claimed the police threatened Miranda and forced his confession. Miranda, he said, was denied consultation with a lawyer and did not know his rights.

The case went to the Supreme Court. In 1966, the justices supported Miranda's claim by a 5–4 vote. The suspect's confession had been obtained illegally, said Chief Justice Earl Warren. Warren put new limits on the power of police to question suspects. A new trial was ordered.

---

6. acquittal: a verdict of "not guilty."

Have you ever known of someone who had a lawyer appointed by the court? Why do you think Gideon fired his court-appointed lawyer? What problems do you think could arise when the court appoints lawyers?

Under the Court's ruling, nothing arrested persons say can be used against them unless police inform them of certain rights: the right to remain silent, the right to a court-appointed attorney, and the right to have an attorney present during questioning. Once they are told of those rights, arrested persons must also be told that, from that point on, anything they say can be used against them.

Thus were born the famous "Miranda rights." Ever since, police across the country have been issued "Miranda cards" containing the phrases they must read to suspects upon arrest. "You have the right to remain silent" and "Anything you say can be used against you" have been heard on countless TV shows as the villain is being handcuffed.

Civil rights advocates praised the decision. They said it helps remind police that criminal suspects, however lowly they may seem, are still human beings with civil rights. But many police were frustrated by the ruling. It limited the evidence they could use in court.

Throughout the 1980s, the Reagan administration sought to overturn the Miranda decision. And, in fact, the courts have chipped away at Miranda. They have made it easier for police to obtain convictions.

As for Miranda himself, he received a new trial. He was reconvicted of kidnapping and rape. The state paroled him in 1972. He drifted through the Southwest, occasionally autographing "Miranda cards" for money. He died in 1976—stabbed over a card game in a Phoenix bar.

 Final Check-in

Have you ever heard about someone being treated unfairly by the police? In what ways do you think Miranda rights should protect people who are arrested?

After You Read

A. Comprehension Check

1. Why couldn't Linda Brown go to the nearby public school?

   _____

   _____

2. What did Linda's father do when Linda was rejected from Sumner?

   _____

   _____

3. What was the Supreme Court's decision in *Gideon v. Wainwright?*

   _____

   _____

4. What are the three "Miranda rights"? _____

   _____

   _____

5. What does the term *to overturn* mean in the sentence, "Throughout the 1980s, the Reagan administration sought *to overturn* the Miranda decision"?
   (1) to overrun   (3) to strengthen
   (2) to reverse   (4) to undermine

B. Revisit the Reading Strategy Discuss your prior knowledge of the first case, *Brown v. Board of Education,* 1954. Do you or anyone in your family remember what schools were like before the end of forced segregation? What were segregated schools like for each race?

C. Think Beyond the Reading Think about these questions and discuss them with a partner. Answer the questions in writing if you wish.

1. What does "separate but equal" mean to you?
2. Do you think everyone is entitled to "due process of law"?
3. What is your opinion of "Miranda rights"?

Think About It: Apply Information

You have just read three accounts of Supreme Court cases. Now you may want to **apply the information** you learned to your own life. Think about how these rulings affect our lives today.

A. Look at Applying Information

Read the following excerpt from the article and answer the question.

> ... the Supreme Court voted 9–0 in favor of Brown. It was a major victory for the civil rights movement. The Court agreed that forced segregation "generates a feeling of inferiority" among minorities. It rejected the concept of "separate but equal" facilities—a rule that had stood since 1892.

How does the 1954 *Brown v. Board of Education* ruling affect us today?

_____

Because of this ruling, public schools are no longer segregated. The ruling has affected the lives of all public school students.

B. Practice Read this excerpt and answer the question.

> The panel voted 9–0 in favor of Gideon. "It is intolerable in a nation which proclaims equal justice under the law . . . that anyone should be handicapped in defending himself simply because he happens to be poor," the Court said. From then on, all people accused of crimes were entitled to legal representation.

How does the 1963 *Gideon v. Wainwright* ruling affect us today? _____

_____

> **Talk About It**
> Discuss which of the three decisions
> • directly affects the most people in the U.S. and why
> • directly affects the fewest people in the U.S. and why
> • most directly affects your life and why
> • has the least effect on your life and why

Write About It: Write Your Opinion

The court cases covered in the article you read affect the lives of many people. Choose the case that interests you most and write a paragraph explaining your opinions. Use one of the following questions as your paragraph topic, or choose a topic of your own.

Brown v. Board of Education: What is your opinion of racially integrated schools?
Gideon v. Wainwright: Can a poor defendant get a fair trial?
Miranda v. Arizona: What do you think it is like to be questioned by the police?

A. **Prewriting** Before you start writing, organize your ideas in the idea frame below. First, write your topic on the top line. Then write your opinion about the topic as a topic sentence. Fill in a reason for your opinion. Next, fill in phrases to remind you about personal experiences and other background knowledge that support or explain your opinion. Then think of other reasons and supporting information and write them in the frame.

Idea Frame

Topic _____

Topic sentence _____

Reason _____

Supporting information _____

Reason _____

Supporting information _____

B. **Writing** Write a paragraph that clearly explains your opinions on the topic. Use your idea frame. Decide which reasons and supporting information you want to use. Decide in which order to use them. Then write a draft of your paragraph.

▶ **Save your draft.** At the end of this unit, you will choose one of your drafts to work with further.

Life Skill: Read a Bar Graph

The saying "A picture is worth a thousand words" is also true of graphs. Graphs are used in place of words to display certain kinds of information. **Bar graphs** are especially helpful when you want to show comparisons.

The bar graph below shows the numbers of lawyers in the U.S. for selected years between 1980 and 1991. Notice that there are two bars for each year on this graph. The key tells us that the blue bar represents male lawyers and the gray bar represents female lawyers. Years are shown along the left side of the graph. Numbers of lawyers are shown at the bottom of the graph.

To read the graph, first choose a year, such as 1980. See where the blue bar for 1980 stops. Estimate the number of male lawyers in 1980, using the numbers on the bottom of the graph. Now estimate the number of female lawyers for the same year, using the gray bar.

There were about 500,000 male and almost 50,000 female lawyers in 1980.

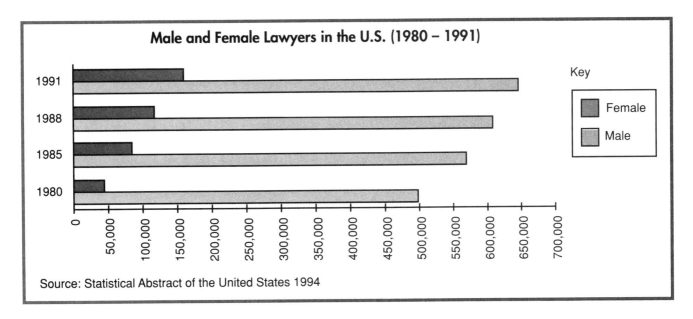

Practice Answer these questions about the graph.

1. About how many female lawyers were there in 1991? _____

2. How did the number of male and female lawyers change over the years

   shown? _____

3. How does the number of female lawyers compare with the number of male

   lawyers in any year? _____

Lesson 11

LEARNING GOALS

Strategy: Set a purpose
Reading: Read a political cartoon and letters to the editor
Skill: Identify the main idea
Writing: Write a letter to the editor
Life Skill: Analyze a political cartoon

Before You Read

In this lesson, you will read a political cartoon and letters to the editor of a newspaper. Although a political cartoon uses humor to make its point, it is not necessarily funny in the way other cartoons are. A political cartoon expresses the cartoonist's opinion about a political issue. The cartoon in this lesson shows a scene of violence that is a part of daily life for many people in the United States. The cartoon makes its point about violence in a dramatic way.

On page 122, you will find sample letters that might have been written to the editor of newspapers that published the cartoon. These letters are typical responses to the ideas expressed in political cartoons.

To set a purpose for reading, decide what you want to learn from the cartoon and the letters. For example, your purpose may be to compare your opinions with those expressed in the cartoon. Or it may be to find out how the writers feel about the cartoon. Do any of their views reflect yours?

To **set your purpose** for reading, choose a question you'd like answered from the ones below, or write your own.

_____ Do I agree with the opinion expressed in the cartoon?

_____ Do most of the letters agree with the cartoon's message?

_____ Do any of the writers mention the effect of violence on young children?

Preview the Reading

Look at the cartoon. What is happening? Now read the first sentence of each letter to the editor. Which letters do you predict will agree with the cartoon? Which do you predict will not like the cartoon?

▶ **Use the Strategy**

In the political cartoon and the letters that follow, opinions are forcefully expressed. Keep in mind the purpose you set as you read.

Americans Held Hostage

AMERICANS HELD HOSTAGE

The people in the cartoon are hiding on the floor in their own house. Discuss these questions to understand the meaning of the cartoon.

1. Where are these people being held hostage?

2. What do the words on the window mean? Why is the window cracked and broken?

3. Why are the people hiding?

4. Notice the newspaper on the floor in the picture. What does the headline say? How does the headline explain what is happening in the cartoon?

5. Read the caption under the cartoon. Where are the Americans being held hostage? What or who is causing them to feel like hostages?

6. Have you ever been "held hostage" in your home by outside violence?

LETTERS TO THE EDITOR

Note from the Editor: The cartoon "Americans Held Hostage" in the October 24 issue brought a larger-than-usual response from our readers. We don't have space to print all the replies, but here are some samples.

Your cartoon "Americans Held Hostage" does not look like my neighborhood at all. I'm sick and tired of all the emphasis on what's wrong with this country. I live in a neighborhood where everyone knows each other. We have neighbor patrols that walk the streets every night. The police can't do it all. It takes work, but our neighborhood helps itself.

Yolanda Green

I could really relate to your October 24 political cartoon about violence in the neighborhood. Just last month, I was robbed at gunpoint as I walked home from the bus stop. I will never feel safe again, knowing that anybody I pass on the street could have a gun. Thanks for letting me express my fears.

Joanna Lyons

Your violent cartoon on October 24 made me sick. Enough of these violent cartoons. I need some real humor to start my day. There must be something funny left in the world.

Pedro Silva

People should take your October 24 cartoon about crime in neighborhoods seriously. We should work on the crime problem through a teenage mentor program. What good is it to moan around and keep saying, "Isn't it awful?" If everyone took time to be friends with just one teenager, that would be a start. If you are interested in helping, call our organization at 555-1212.

Steve Forseyth
Youth Mentor Program

There is another side to the crime shown in your cartoon of October 24. I'm the mother of a young man in jail. That jail is terribly overcrowded. The whole message is punish, punish. He needs to learn some skills. He has no skills. He has no way to earn money. What good is punishment going to do for him? How will that keep him out of trouble?

Stella Washington

After You Read

A. Comprehension Check Check whether each statement is **True** or **False**.

True   **False**

_____ _____   **1.** The cartoon shows Americans overseas.

_____ _____   **2.** The cracks in the window represent bullet holes.

_____ _____   **3.** There were many replies to the cartoon.

_____ _____   **4.** One writer wrote from his jail cell.

_____ _____   **5.** All the writers expressed fear about violent crime.

_____ _____   **6.** One writer was a recent victim of crime.

_____ _____   **7.** All the replies were printed in the paper.

_____ _____   **8.** The first writer agreed with the cartoon.

_____ _____   **9.** The second writer feels that crime is down.

_____ _____   **10.** Pedro Silva wants cartoons that make him laugh.

B. Revisit the Reading Strategy Look again at the purpose you set before you read the cartoon and letters. Discuss the following questions with a partner.

1. Did setting a purpose help you find out certain information?
2. Were you able to get more out of your reading?

C. Think Beyond the Reading Think about these questions and discuss them with a partner. Answer the questions in writing if you wish.

1. Compare the power of a political cartoon with a letter on the same subject.
2. Why do you think cartoons are often used to portray hotly debated topics?
3. Why do you think people write letters to the editors of newspapers?
4. If you were an editor of a newspaper, how would you choose which letters to print? What criteria would you use?

Think About It: Identify the Main Idea

The **main idea** is the most important point of a piece of writing. The main idea is what the piece is all about. Often the main idea is stated in the first or second sentence, but it can also be in the middle or at the end of a piece of writing. Sometimes the main idea is not actually stated in the piece. Then you have to figure out the main idea by reading the piece as a whole.

A. Look at Identifying the Main Idea

> People should take your October 24 cartoon about crime in neighborhoods seriously. We should work on the crime problem through a teenage mentor program. What good is it to moan around and keep saying, "Isn't it awful?" If everyone took time to be friends with just one teenager, that would be a start. If you are interested in helping, call our organization at 555-1212.
>
> Steve Forseyth
> Youth Mentor Program

1. In the letter at left, one of the sentences states the main idea, but it is not the first sentence. Read the letter and think about the main point the writer makes. Then underline the sentence that states the main idea of the letter.

   You should have underlined the second sentence, "We should work on the crime problem through a teenage mentor program." The letter is about the teenage mentor program.

> There is another side to the crime shown in your cartoon of October 24. I'm the mother of a young man in jail. That jail is terribly overcrowded. The whole message is punish, punish. He needs to learn some skills. He has no skills. He has no way to earn money. What good is punishment going to do for him? How will that keep him out of trouble?
>
> Stella Washington

2. In the next example, the main idea is not stated. Read the letter and figure out the main point. Then write the main idea in your own words below.

   Main idea: _____

   _____

   _____

   The main idea is that punishment will not stop crime. You could also say that the main idea is that skills will keep her son from crime.

B. Practice Below are three more sample letters to the editor about the October 24 cartoon. Read each letter. For letters 1 and 2, underline the sentence that states the main idea of the letter. For letter 3, write the main idea in your own words.

1. I am writing because of your October 24 cartoon about crime. My neighborhood has cleaned out the drug gangs. It took a lot of work, but we did it. Mothers with their babies and kids on their bikes have reclaimed our sidewalks and streets. We worked at it every minute of every day, and we did it.

   Lucy Sanchez

2. Your October 24 crime cartoon makes me miss the old days. I can remember a time when everybody in our neighborhood left the doors unlocked. If my next door neighbor needed to borrow some milk, she would just walk in, take some milk, and leave a little note. It's too bad we can't turn back the clock. We were all much safer 40 years ago.

   Sam Reston

3. Your crime cartoon of October 24 did not scare me a bit. If the criminals succeeded in scaring me, then I wouldn't be able to go where I want, when I want. I won't change my lifestyle just because someone else can't obey the law. I don't even give criminals a thought.

   Karen White

Main idea _____

 Talk About It

Crime in America is a hotly debated topic for many people. Some opinions on this topic are listed below. With a partner, pick one of these opinions and clearly state why you agree or disagree with it. Then give reasons for why you feel that way. Listen as your partner does the same.

1. Laws against gun ownership don't keep guns out of criminals' hands.
2. Prisoners deserve strict punishment and no education or training.
3. Teenage mentor programs might reduce teenage crime.

Write About It: Write a Letter to the Editor

Letters to the editor are one way people can show concern about issues. You too can write a letter to the editor of your local paper. Choose an issue that has something to do with crime or the law, such as a topic from this lesson.

A. **Prewriting** Before you write, explore and organize your thoughts on the topic. Use an idea frame like you used in Lesson 10. Write your topic on the first line. Fill in the rest of the frame. Then use your ideas to write a letter to the editor.

Idea Frame

Topic _____

Topic sentence _____

Reason _____

Supporting information _____

Reason _____

Supporting information _____

B. **Writing** Write a letter to the editor of your newspaper on the topic you chose. Use your idea frame.

- Start by stating the topic or problem that your letter is about.
- Decide which reasons and supporting information you want to use.
- Decide the order in which to use them.
- Draft your letter.

Your letter doesn't have to be long. Many of the best letters are brief, but they clearly state the writer's opinion.

▶ **Save your draft.** At the end of this unit, you will choose one of your drafts to work with further.

Life Skill: Analyze a Political Cartoon

As you learned in this lesson, a political cartoon is an expression of the cartoonist's opinion about a current political issue or event. Political cartoons are usually found on the editorial page of the newspaper.

Political cartoons often contain symbols. For instance, a picture of "Uncle Sam" frequently represents the United States. Symbols may be labeled to show what they represent.

When you read a political cartoon, first decide what the symbols represent. Then read the title, the captions, and the labels. Ask yourself, "What is the cartoonist saying about this topic?"

In the cartoon below, what does the human figure represent?

The figure is wearing a long black robe like a judge's robe. It is labeled "Justice." The figure represents the U.S. justice system.

Practice Answer these questions about the political cartoon on a separate paper.

1. What is the title of this cartoon?
2. What is "Justice" carrying?
3. Does "Justice" seem to be steady on his feet?
4. What is the cartoonist saying about the U.S. justice system?

 Talk About It

Look for political cartoons in your local newspapers. Bring in one or more that interest you and discuss them with a partner or a small group.

Lesson 12

> **LEARNING GOALS**
>
> **Strategy:** Visualize
> **Reading:** Read a story
> **Skill:** Follow a sequence of events
> **Writing:** Write a poem
> **Life Skill:** Read a parking ticket

Before You Read

In this lesson a policeman tells about an unusual sequence of events that happened during a robbery.

Before you begin to read, **visualize,** or picture in your mind, a small convenience store.

- Compare your image of the inside of a typical convenience store with a big supermarket.
- Now imagine how a small store can be an easy target for a robbery.

Preview the Reading

To preview the story, look at the picture and read the first two sentences of the story. This will set the stage for the officer's story. What do you predict will happen?

▶ **Use the Strategy**

To better understand this reading, visualize the setting and each action as it takes place.

Crimebusters

Mark Baker

We got a report from a confidential informant[1] that one of these little Jiffy Marts was going to be held up on a Sunday morning. So we staked the place out. It was built in such a way that it faced the hard road, but on either end and in the back of it was wooded area. The nearest business or house was maybe 300 or 400 yards away. There was no back door to this building, so the only way to come out was through the front door. The lady inside didn't even know that we were staking it out. I was directly across the street in plainclothes and I had a walkie-talkie and was supposed to alert the others if something happened so they could close in.

About five minutes after nine, I saw this fellow park his car about 50 feet away from the building and raise the hood to make motorists think that he was broke down. He came walking up kind of stiff-legged and I could see with binoculars that he had what looked like a rifle or shotgun in his pants leg.

We waited till he got in good and I could see the lady putting the money in a bag. Then he pushed her into the cooler in the back. I was telling all these other fellows what was happening on the radio. We were set to move.

Check-in ▶ Visualize what has just happened. Where is the woman who works at the store? Where are the plainclothes police?

About that time a car pulled up right behind this fellow's car and a man got out. He had his hand inside his shirt. He goes easing up to the Jiffy Mart. Inside, the first robber puts the shotgun back in his pants, got the bag of money situated real good under his arm and he was walking to the front of the store. The other fellow had gotten onto the concrete within two or three feet of the door. That's where they met. The second gunman pulled out his pistol and put it

---

1. confidential informant: a person who provides information to police secretly.

into the first robber's face and backed him into the store. The first man dropped the bag of money and got put in the cooler with the woman clerk.

When Number Two comes back up front to pick up the money, he was told not to move or he will be blowed to bits, because there was three of us there with the drop on him. He dropped his pistol and his money. We put handcuffs on him. Then we go to the cooler. Number One comes out and we put handcuffs on him and grab his gun out of his britches leg. The girl is, of course, really upset and scared. We call her husband and get her taken care of.

In the meantime, we tell the two robbers their rights and that we're going to put them in jail for armed robbery and grand larceny and a couple of other things. The first one turned to us and said with a straight face, "I'd like to prefer charges, too."

"For what?"

"Against the man who come in and held me up."

▶ **Final Check-in**
Did visualizing the setting and sequence of this unusual robbery help you to understand what was going on? Were you able to imagine the scene? Were there any events you could *not* visualize? Reread those parts and see if you can visualize them now.

With a partner or small group, discuss these questions about the cartoon below and the story "Crimebusters." How is the robber in this cartoon acting like the first robber at the end of "Crimebusters"? It seems as though both robbers want to break the law, but they both also want the protection of the law. Do you think that people who commit crimes should be protected by the law? Why or why not?

After You Read

A. Comprehension Check

1. Who reported that a Jiffy Mart would be held up?

    (1) the owner of the Jiffy Mart
    (2) a confidential informant
    (3) a policeman in a cruiser
    (4) a neighbor of the Jiffy Mart

2. What did the author mean when he wrote, "So we staked the place out"?

    (1) They put a fence around the Jiffy Mart.
    (2) They surrounded the Jiffy Mart.
    (3) They opened the place up.
    (4) They watched the place from a distance.

3. The police officer was ready to move in on the robbery scene, but

    (1) a shot rang out
    (2) another robber arrived
    (3) the clerk ran out of the store
    (4) the police backup didn't show up

4. Why was the first robber's request at the end of the story funny?

    (1) He was a robber who was robbed.
    (2) He was an innocent bystander.
    (3) He used a pistol, not a shotgun.
    (4) He thought the policemen were robbers, too.

B. Revisit the Reading Strategy

Earlier you visualized how a small store could be easily robbed. Did anything you visualized about the Jiffy Mart in this story make it seem easy to rob? Share your thoughts with a partner or your instructor.

C. Think Beyond the Reading

Think about these questions and discuss them with a partner. Answer the questions in writing if you wish.

Have you or anyone you know ever been robbed? What happened? How did you or the robbery victim feel?

Think About It: Follow a Sequence of Events

The **sequence of events** in a story is the order in which things happen. It tells how the story begins, the order in which events take place, and how the story ends. When the events are related in order, it is usually easy to understand a story.

Time-related words such as *when, just as, then, next,* and *finally* can help you follow the sequence of events and understand a story.

A. Look at Following a Sequence of Events

Read the following paragraph from the account in this lesson. Notice that each event is numbered.

When [1]Number Two comes back up front to pick up the money, [2]he was told not to move or he will be blowed to bits, because there was three of us there with the drop on him. [3]He dropped his pistol and his money. [4]We put handcuffs on him. [5]Then we go to the cooler. [6]Number One comes out and [7]we put handcuffs on him and [8]grab his gun out of his britches leg.

Here are the eight events listed in order:
1. Number Two comes back up front.
2. He was told not to move.
3. He dropped his pistol and his money.
4. We put handcuffs on him.
5. Then we go to the cooler.
6. Number One comes out.
7. We put handcuffs on him.
8. [We] grab his gun out of his britches leg.

B. Practice Read the paragraph below. Number the events in the paragraph. Then list the events in the order in which they happened. You can put them into your own words. The first and last events are listed for you.

 About that time a car pulled up right behind this fellow's car and a man got out. He had his hand inside his shirt. He goes easing up to the Jiffy Mart. Inside, the first robber puts the shotgun back in his pants, got the bag of money situated real good under his arm and he was walking to the front of the store. The other fellow had gotten onto the concrete within two or three feet of the door. That's where they met. The second gunman pulled out his pistol and put it into the first robber's face and backed him into the store. The first man dropped the bag of money and got put in the cooler with the woman clerk.

1. A car pulled up behind this fellow's car.

2. _____

3. _____

4. _____

5. _____

6. _____

7. _____

8. _____

9. _____

10. _____

11. _____

12. The first man got put in the cooler.

▶ **Talk About It**
With a partner or a small group, retell the story about the Jiffy Mart robbery. Include enough details to clearly explain this fast-moving sequence of events. Be sure to include the funny ending when Robber Number One makes an unexpected request.

Write About It: Write a Poem

Crime and the law are issues that can affect our lives deeply. Such issues inspire writers to write about their experiences and their feelings. The following poem, written by Stewart Brisby while in prison, describes how he feels about prison life.

Poems are carefully constructed pieces of writing. Poets choose words to create images that produce emotional reactions in readers. As you read "The Artist," visualize what the poet is describing. How does the poem make you feel?

The Artist

Stewart Brisby

funny (or not so)
how a man in prison
thinks of all the things
he should have done
the things
he meant to say.

he writes letters
but a letter
cannot warm a bed
kiss a child.

so at night
in a double-edged cubicle
sleep
makes him an artist
& he paints
the water color world
he remembers.

but in the morning
he must take the easel
out to dry

& it is raining
in the prison yard.

What images did you visualize as you read the poem?
How did the poem make you feel?

Poetry can be written in many different forms. Poetry often involves rhyme and a specific rhythm pattern. "The Artist," however, has no specific rhyme or rhythm patterns. This form of poetry is called **free verse**. In free verse, as in all forms of poetry, the words are carefully chosen and carefully placed on the page to evoke images and emotional reactions.

A. Prewriting Try writing a free verse poem of your own. First reread "The Artist." Look at the images the poet selected and the words he chose to express those images. Notice how he placed words on the page. Think about why he chose to use only lowercase letters and very short lines.

Then choose a topic. Think about the ideas you want to express in your poem. Brainstorm some images you might use to express those ideas and some words to convey those images. Try to think of descriptive words that bring strong images to mind.

B. Writing Now draft your poem. Make it as long or as short as you'd like.

Remember
- There is no exact pattern you have to follow.
- Lines can be long or short. Capitalization and punctuation rules can be ignored.
- Words have power. Choose words that evoke strong images and emotional reactions.

Use this as the start of your poem, or make up a beginning yourself.

In My Dreams

Every night _____

_____

_____

But the next day _____

_____

▶ **Save your draft.** At the end of this unit, you will choose one of your drafts to work with further.

Life Skill: Read a Parking Ticket

Parking violations are among the most common crimes people are charged with. Most people pay their fines promptly. Some people don't take parking tickets seriously. Failure to pay fines may result in your driver's license not being renewed. If you receive a parking ticket, you must be sure to read it carefully to know what to do.

VIOLATION				
NO.	MONTH	DAY	YEAR	

STATE

PLATE
COLOR	TYPE		REGISTRATION
☐ G	☐ PA		
	☐ CO		
☐ R	☐ OTHER		

VEHICLE MAKE	VEHICLE COLOR

LOCATION	METER NO.

OFFICER NAME	BADGE NO.	TIME	FROM	TO
			AM	AM
I HAVE AFFIXED THIS NOTICE TO VEHICLE			PM	PM

PARKING CLERK COPY

☐ A1 METER VIOLATION	$5		☐ B9 WITHIN 20 FT OF INTERSECTION	$10
☐ A2 OVERTIME PARKING VIOLATION - 20 MIN.	$5		☐ B10 UPON A STREET OR HIGHWAY POSTED NO PARKING	$10
☐ A3 OVERTIME PARKING VIOLATION - ONE HOUR	$5		☐ B11 BUS STOP OR TAXI STAND	$10
☐ A4 OVERTIME PARKING VIOLATION - TWO HOURS	$5		☐ B12 LOADING ZONE	$10
☐ B1 WITHIN AN INTERSECTION	$10		☐ B13 IMPROPER ANGLE PARKING	$10
☐ B2 UPON A SIDEWALK	$10		☐ B14 SAFETY ZONE	$10
☐ B3 UPON A CROSSWALK	$10		☐ B15 RESTRICTED PLACE	$10
☐ B4 RIGHT TIRE OVER 1 FT FROM CURB	$10		☐ B16 WRONG DIRECTION	$10
☐ B5 LESS THAN 10 FT. FROM OBSTRUCTED LANE	$10		☐ B17 RESIDENT PERMIT PARKING	$10
☐ B6 UPON A ROADWAY IN A RURAL DISTRICT	$10		☐ B18 DOUBLE PARKING	$10
			☐ B19 FIRE LANE	$10
☐ B7 WITHIN 10 FT OF A HYDRANT	$10		☐ C1 ALL NIGHT PARKING	$15
			☐ C2 SNOW REMOVAL	$15
☐ B8 UPON A PRIVATE ROAD OR ACROSS A DRIVEWAY	$10		☐ C3 HANDICAP SPACE OR CURB RAMP	$15
			☐ D1 OTHER	$ ___

PAY THIS AMOUNT $5 ☐ $10 ☐ $15 ☐

This notice must be returned with payment to the office of the parking clerk. Hours 8:30 A.M. to 4:30 P.M. Pay by mail, personally, or by an authorized person. A hearing may be obtained upon written request of the registered owner.

If this notice is not paid within 21 days from the date of violation, the fine for Group A violations will increase from $5.00 to $7.00. Failure to pay on any violation will result in the non-renewal of the driver's license and registration of the registered owner.

DO NOT MAIL CASH, pay only by POSTAL NOTE, MONEY ORDER, or BANK CHECK.

To answer these sample questions, look at the left-hand column on the parking ticket:

What have you done wrong if A2 is checked on the ticket? _____

_____

How much is the fine for A2? _____

If you answered "parked 20 minutes too long" and "$5," you read the ticket correctly.

Practice Answer these questions about the parking ticket.

1. What will happen if fines from Group A violations are not paid within 21 days?

   _____

2. How far are you supposed to park from a fire hydrant?

   _____

3. Can you mail cash to pay the fine? _____

4. What will happen if the car owner never pays a parking ticket?

   _____

   _____

►Writing Skills Mini-Lesson: Using Apostrophes Correctly

An **apostrophe** (') is a punctuation mark that is used for two different purposes:

1. **To form a *contraction*** Put the apostrophe in place of the missing letters.

   It is the law ➡ It's the law.   Do not steal ➡ Don't steal.

2. **To form a *possessive noun***
   - **If the noun is singular,** add an apostrophe and the letter *s* ('s).
     The store of the man ➡ The man's store
     The rim of the glass ➡ The glass's rim
   - **If the noun is plural,** add an apostrophe after the *s* ending (s').
     The car of the robbers ➡ The robbers' car
   - **If the plural noun doesn't end in *s*,** add apostrophe *s*. ('s)
     The voice of the people ➡ The people's voice

Tip   Do not add an apostrophe
   - to form possessive pronouns: *its, hers, yours, ours, theirs.*
   - to form a plural noun.
     Wrong: Violence can leave it's victim's fearful.
     Right: Violence can leave its victims fearful.

Practice Copy this paragraph on separate paper. Add apostrophes where they belong.

Last year, Katrina Smiths car was stolen. The police found it,

but its hubcaps were missing. Now Katrinas car has an alarm. Its

very loud, and it sometimes goes off when other peoples cars get

too close to it. Even childrens bicycles can set it off. The

neighbors dont like it at all. Katrina is concerned about her

neighbors complaints, but shes worried about her car, too.

▶Unit 4 Review

Reading Review

From Treasure to Trash ▮▮▮▮▮▮▮▮▮▮▮▮▮▮

It's too bad we don't know when tragedy is going to strike so we can change our plans. That must be how Nancy and Mark Lee feel, now that it's too late. Their story starts on a Saturday morning in July. They had spent the entire week organizing and labeling things to sell at a garage sale.

The Lees were at a difficult point in their lives. They needed money to make the last payment on their car. Making the car payment was important to them. Mark needed a car to get to work, no matter how old and beat up it was. It was hard to get jobs; Mark needed to keep his.

Mark and Nancy had been laying out items for sale since early morning in order to be ready for customers by nine o'clock. They had filled their tiny front yard with goods in the shape of a large letter *U*. Dishes, some old pots and pans, and a few appliances were laid out at the back of the *U* near their front door. Along one side they had propped up makeshift tables on which were neatly folded sweaters, jeans, and children's outgrown coats and shoes. On the other side of the *U* was some of their sports equipment— which they hated to sell, but they needed the money more—and some of the children's games.

Mark heard the sound of the police siren first. Then Nancy heard it and saw a brown Lincoln Continental speeding just yards ahead of the police car at the beginning of their block. From then on, everything seemed to happen in slow motion, though it took only seconds. As it approached their yard, the Lincoln skidded into a parked car. Then it veered toward Mark and Nancy. They ran blindly into the neighbors' yard without looking back. But they could hear the sounds of dishes breaking and metal crunching. They knew without looking that their belongings—and their garage sale—had been destroyed.

Police quickly surrounded the driver. He was not going anywhere else in this stolen car. It was amazing that he was not hurt. Mark and Nancy were in shock as they filled out the police report. They hoped to get some insurance money for their damaged possessions. But they couldn't claim the damage done to their finances. Ironically, a car thief had ruined their hopes of paying off an honestly acquired car—at least for this month.

1. Number the events below in the order in which they happened.

   _____ A brown Lincoln skids into a parked car.

   _____ Mark and Nancy lay out items for their garage sale.

   _____ Police surround the driver of the Lincoln.

   _____ A police siren is heard.

   _____ Mark and Nancy fill out a police report.

   _____ The brown Lincoln destroys Mark and Nancy's garage sale.

2. Reread the second paragraph of the story. What is the main idea?

   (1) The car is old and beat up.   (3) Mark and Nancy are having a hard time.

   (2) Mark and Nancy need to own a car.   (4) Mark and Nancy need to get a better car.

Writing Process

In Unit 4 you wrote three first drafts. Choose the piece that you would like to work with further. You will revise, edit, and make a final copy of this draft.

   _____ your opinion about a court decision (page 118)

   _____ your letter to the editor (page 126)

   _____ your poem (page 136)

Find the first draft you chose. Then turn to page 160 in this book. Follow steps 3, 4, and 5 in the Writing Process to create a final draft.

As you revise, check your draft for this specific point:

Opinion: Be sure to include specific reasons to support your opinion.

Letter: Remember to stay on the topic.

Poem: Keep in mind that every word counts.

Skills Review

This review will let you see how well you can use the skills taught in this book. When you have finished Units 1–4, complete this review. Then share your work with your instructor.

Reading Skills

Read each passage and answer the questions that follow.

The World's Easiest Workout

Daryn Eller

What if we told you that there's a way you can get fit and stay fit while barely raising a sweat? A miracle method that doesn't require going to the gym, exercising to a video or spending a lot of money? It may sound like a dream, but it isn't. In fact, it's something you already know how to do: walking.

Think of the facts about this body-slimming, fat-burning activity. Walking can offer you a serious calorie burn-off, depending on your weight and how fast you go. If a 150-pound woman walks three miles in 60 minutes, for instance, she'll knock off 240 calories. At four miles an hour, she'll burn 350 calories. If she ups her pace to four and a half miles in that time, she'll drop 440 calories in an hour.

How do you get started? Start by walking three times a week for 20 minutes, says Carol Espel, a national Walk Reebok instructor and program director at Apex gym in New York City. Once you feel at ease with this level of intensity—a few weeks should do it—add more days per week to increase calorie burning. Then up your mileage by 5 to 10 percent per week. For example, if you're now walking two miles, next week add one tenth or two tenths of a mile more. Finally, quicken your pace bit by bit. In time you should be walking at a faster mile-per-hour rate for longer periods. For the best results, wear sneakers made for walking. Swing your arms naturally but energetically with your elbows bent at 90-degree angles. Maintain good posture. Keep your shoulders back but relaxed. Hold your head high.

Here are 10 more good reasons to start walking now.

1. You're more likely to stick with it than with other exercise programs. A number of studies back this up.
2. It will tone, shape, and strengthen your legs—thighs, calves and all.
3. Your tush will tighten up.
4. Like most exercises, walking reduces stress. It brings on feelings of general well-being.
5. You'll strengthen your bones. Walking has been shown to increase bone density. This helps stave off osteoporosis.
6. It's an exercise that doesn't cause injury or pain. This is especially true if you warm up your body by walking slowly for a few minutes and cool down exactly the same way.
7. Your energy level will increase.
8. You can invite others to do it with you—friends, kids, spouse. You don't have to go it alone.
9. Walking on a regular basis can reduce your risk of heart disease.
10. You can easily fit walking into your life. You can walk on the way to work, after dinner, around the mall or the neighborhood. You can walk just about anytime, anywhere.

Choose the best answer to each question.

1. What is the main idea of this article?
   (1) Walking burns off calories.
   (2) Walking does not cost money.
   (3) Walking will help you stay fit.
   (4) Walking does not cause injury.

2. What's so easy about walking?
   (1) You can use a video.
   (2) You can walk anywhere.
   (3) You can use an exercise machine.
   (4) You can go to a gym.

3. What is the correct way to begin exercise walking?
   (1) Walk three times a week for 20 minutes.
   (2) Walk until you feel a little tired.
   (3) Walk a little every day.
   (4) Walk faster to burn calories.

4. What problem can walking help you solve?
   (1) high energy level
   (2) too much stress
   (3) kidney disease
   (4) too much bone density

5. To build walking into your life, you can
   (1) join a new gym
   (2) always walk alone
   (3) walk only indoors
   (4) increase distance and speed bit by bit

6. For best results, you should
   (1) hold your arms at your side
   (2) start by running in place
   (3) maintain good posture
   (4) walk only in the morning

The Floor Mopper

Gary A. Franks

Gary A. Franks was elected a Republican congressman from Connecticut in 1990.

"Be proud of what you do," my father always told me, "whether you're boss or mopping floors."

When I was 17, I got a summer job at Waterbury Hospital Health Center in Waterbury, Conn. I was told my duties would include mopping floors. I smiled and remembered Dad's advice.

Even though my job was the lowest, I was thrilled to have any work at all. Each morning, I imagined all the sick people not being able to eat if I wasn't there to scrub the pots coated with oatmeal. After breakfast, I cleaned toilets. In the late afternoon, I mopped floors. Though I was dead tired, I knew that if the floors didn't shine, it would reflect badly on me. I wanted people to say, "That young man sure does a nice job."

Working at the hospital taught me that it takes people on every level, from pot scrubber to CEO, working as one, for an organization to function well. I understood this and never had a problem being motivated.

Through every job I've ever held, my father's wise words have stayed with me. I've mopped floors, and I've been the boss. I think Dad would be proud.

Choose the best answer to each question.

7. What was Gary Franks's main message?
   (1) Everyone should start by mopping floors.
   (2) On any job, be proud of your work.
   (3) To be a boss is the most important job.
   (4) Low level jobs don't matter.

8. What effect did the summer job in the hospital have on Franks?
   (1) He enjoyed physical labor.
   (2) He was thrilled to have the job.
   (3) He learned that some jobs are not important.
   (4) He questioned his father's advice.

Should All Criminals Go to Jail?

Many people in the U.S. feel that crime is the country's number one problem. As a result, many Americans support tough laws for sentencing criminals. They say these tough laws are paying off. They say that tough punishment prevents crime.

Many Europeans take a different view. Punishment, they say, does not prevent crime. They feel government should work on the roots of crime. Solving social problems like poverty and racism is the only way to reduce crime, they say.

Not surprisingly, Americans and Europeans have different views about crimes that deserve a jail term. Many Americans support jail terms for those convicted of nonviolent crimes, such as theft. Many Europeans do not.

These views can be seen in the chart below.

Should a Person Go to Jail for Stealing a TV?	
Country	**Percent who said "Yes"**
Switzerland	8.5%
Germany	12.4%
Norway	12.4%
France	13.2%
Netherlands	26.7%
England	39.2%
United States	55.3%

Choose the best answer to each question.

9. According to the chart, what percent of people in the U.S. support jail terms for the theft of a TV?
(1) 8.5%
(2) 13.2%
(3) 44.7%
(4) 55.3%

10. How would most Europeans solve the problem of crime?
(1) Put all criminals in jail.
(2) Put nonviolent criminals in jail.
(3) Reduce poverty and racism.
(4) Reduce the length of jail sentences.

Writing Skills

On separate paper, copy the paragraph. Correct sentence fragments, run-on sentences, and any mistakes in usage or punctuation.

When Smith School held a fair last week. Many parent's and children took part. The fair is a yearly fund-raising event this year the school will use the money to buy more computer's. The games at the fair this year were the most silliest ever several games drew large crowds. The most popular event was called "Dunk the Doctor." A local doctor volunteered his services to be dunked by kid's throwing balls. The doctors beeper went off. Toward the end of the afternoon. The kids didnt have no more tries to dunk him. The annual fall fair. A fun event for all ages.

Write About It

On separate paper, write about the topic below or choose your own topic. Follow the first four steps of the Writing Process (page 160) to write, revise, and edit your draft. Use the checklist below as you revise. When you have edited your draft, write a final draft.

Topic Many companies hire part-time workers. Most of these workers do not get benefits of any kind. Do you think people who work 20 to 30 hours a week should receive benefits, such as vacation pay, health insurance, or maternity leave? Why or why not? Write one or more paragraphs to explain your opinion.

Revising Checklist

When revising and editing your draft, check to be sure that it

_____ has one main idea in each paragraph

_____ states your opinion at the beginning

_____ gives reasons to support your point of view

_____ includes details or examples to explain your reasons

Skills Review Answers

Reading Skills

1. (3)	**6.** (3)
2. (2)	**7.** (2)
3. (1)	**8.** (2)
4. (2)	**9.** (4)
5. (4)	**10.** (3)

Writing Skills

Here is a possible way to correct the paragraph. Your answer may vary.

When Smith School held a fair last week, many parents and children took part. The fair is a yearly fund-raising event. This year the school will use the money to buy more computers. The games at the fair this year were the silliest ever. Several games drew large crowds. The most popular event was called "Dunk the Doctor." A local doctor volunteered his services to be dunked by kids throwing balls. The doctor's beeper went off toward the end of the afternoon. The kids didn't have any more tries to dunk him. The annual fall fair is a fun event for all ages.

Write About It

When you feel confident about your final draft, share it with your instructor.

Evaluation Chart

Check your Skills Review answers. Then, on the chart below, circle the number of any answer you missed. You may need to review the lessons indicated next to that question number.

Question	Skill	Lesson Numbers
1	main idea	6, 11
2	key facts	5, 9
3	sequence of events	12
4	problems and solutions	1, 7
5	apply information	2, 10
6	cause and effect	3, 4
7	main idea	6, 11
8	cause and effect	3, 4
9	key facts	5, 9
10	problems and solutions	1, 7

Student Self-Assessment

Go to page 148 to complete Student Self-Assessment #2.

Student Self-Assessment #2

After you finish the Skills Review, do this self-assessment.
Share your responses with your instructor.

Reading	Good at this	Improving	Little progress
I can read and understand			
1. stories and poems			
2. articles in magazines, newspapers, and books			
3. pamphlets and brochures			
4. charts and graphs			
5. maps			
6. political cartoons			
When I read, I can			
1. figure out new words by using context clues, and by breaking long words into smaller parts			
2. use what I already know to help me understand			
3. try to predict what is coming next			
4. visualize what I read			
5. find key facts			
6. identify cause and effect relationships			
7. identify problems and solutions in reading selections			
8. follow a set of written directions			
9. apply information I've read to new situations			

Writing	Good at this	Improving	Little progress
I can fill out or write			
1. charts			
2. forms and applications			
3. announcements			
4. songs and poems			
5. journal entries			
6. paragraphs with a topic sentence and supporting details			
7. letters to the editor			
8. directions			
When I write, I can			
1. think of good ideas			
2. organize my ideas			
3. use facts, examples, or reasons to support my main ideas			
4. express myself clearly so others understand			
5. revise my writing to improve it			
6. edit my writing to correct spelling, capitalization, punctuation, and usage errors			
7. recognize fragments and run-on sentences and fix them			

Answer Key

When sample answers are given, your answers may use different wording but should be similar to them.

Unit 1 Staying Healthy

▼ Lesson 1

After You Read (p. 19)

A. Sample answers:
1. She ate candy while watching a TV program.
2. Her mother wouldn't be able to go on the class hike.
3. Her mother was out of shape. Rachel felt her mother didn't take care of herself anymore.
4. Pat realized how much she cared about what her daughter thought of her.

Think About It: Recognize Problems and Solutions (p. 20)

B. Practice

Sample answers:
1. exercise; walk
2. eat fruits and vegetables for snacks
3. eat three healthy meals a day; don't skip meals
4. bring down her blood pressure

Life Skill: Read Medicine Labels (p. 23)

Possible definitions:
1. **indications:** symptoms, or specific health problems
2. **dosage:** specific quantity or amount to take
3. **drug interaction precaution:** warning about harmful effects of mixing certain medicines

Practice

Information will vary. Check with your instructor.

▼ Lesson 2

After You Read (p. 28)

A. 1. False   6. True
   2. True   7. True
   3. False   8. False
   4. False   9. True
   5. False   10. True

Life Skill: A Closer Look at a Food Chart (p. 31)

Practice

1. either bok choy or broccoli
2. yes
3. Vitamin A, fiber
4. no
5. any two of the following: grapefruit, kiwi fruit, orange

▼ Lesson 3

After You Read (p. 37)

A. 1. (4)
   2. (2)
   3. (3)
   4. (2)

Think About It: Understand Cause and Effect (p. 38)

B. Practice

1. **Cause:** Charlie baked the chicken to an internal temperature of 160 degrees
   Effect: completely kill harmful bacteria
   Cue words: in order to
2. **Cause:** meat is not cooked thoroughly
   Effect: E. coli can remain alive in the meat
3. **Cause:** Adnan sets his refrigerator at 40 degrees
   Effect: food in his refrigerator does not become tainted
   Cue words: consequently
4. **Cause:** Liz learned that fish living in warm waters near coral reefs are most likely to be contaminated
   Effect: she avoids eating those fish
   Cue words: therefore
5. **Cause:** Employees did not wash their hands before handling food and dishes.
   Effect: They contaminated the food with bacteria from their hands.
6. **Cause:** Pasteurization kills bacteria
   Effect: pasteurized milk is safer to drink
   Cue words: as a result
7. **Cause:** they may have been sprayed with pesticides
   Effect: Sarah washes fresh fruits and vegetables
   Cue word: because

Write About It: Create a Chart (p. 40)

Sample entries:

Foods	Proper Storage	Preparation Tips	Internal Temperature
hamburger	Wrap securely Store at 40° F or cooler	Cook until center is gray or brown	160° F
frozen fish	Keep frozen at 0° F or colder	Thaw in refrigerator	160° F
raw chicken	Wrap securely Store at 40° F or cooler on lower shelf	Wash hands before and after handling	160° F

▼ Writing Skills Mini-Lesson: Fixing Sentence Fragments (p. 42)

There are different ways to fix the fragments. Here are some examples:

Parents need to feed their children healthy food. Unfortunately, too many children like junk food. They prefer potato chips and cola to carrots and milk. If they eat only junk food, they get sick often. What can parents do? For one thing, they can keep only healthy food in the home. It is wise to start good habits before children are old enough for school.

▼ Unit 1 Review (p. 43)

Reading Review

1. False
2. False
3. False
4. True
5. False
6. True
7. False

Unit 2 Get That Job!

▼ Lesson 4

After You Read (p. 50)

A. Sample answers:

1. Easy job. Good Wages. No experience necessary.
2. a large loft; tubs filled with water; wooden benches
3. Probably not. The foreman wouldn't allow the use of a pen knife or safety razor.
4. They will be less likely to believe some claims made in want ads.

Think About It: Understand Cause and Effect (p. 51)

B. Practice

Sample answers:

1. **cause:** being out of work
   effect: bought newspaper or turned to "Help Wanted—Unskilled" section
2. **cause:** hand in cold water for a long time
   effect: body began to shiver
3. **cause:** the softening did not work uniformly
   effect: pieces of label remained stuck to the bottle
4. **cause:** a painful, swollen finger
   effect: Colon quit the job
5. **cause:** detaching labels from wet bottles
   effect: thumb and nail had become an unnatural tool developed for the job

Life Skill: Interpret Want Ads (p. 55)

1. **trans.**   transportation
   F/T   full-time
   &   and
   P/T   part-time
   Tu.   Tuesday
   Fri.   Friday
   appt.   appointment
2. **Exp.**   experience
   w/   with
   nec.   necessary
   perm.   permanent
   &   and
   temp.   temporary
   Exc.   excellent
   ASAP   as soon as possible
3. **Attn.**   attention
   Exc.   excellent
   Flex.   flexible
   hrs.   hours
   Morn.   morning
   Aft.   afternoon
   Eve.   evening
   immed.   immediately
   exp.   experience
   nec.   necessary

4. **tchr's.**	teacher's
H.S.	high school
G.E.D.	General Educational Development
req.	required
Mon.	Monday
Fri.	Friday
Refs.	references
req.	required

5. ad 3

▼ Lesson 5

After You Read (p. 59)

A. 1. (3) 3. (2)
2. (2) 4. (1)

B. Your height, weight, and favorite color would probably not be factors in doing the job. It is illegal for employers to discriminate on the basis of age, religion, or national origin.

Think About It: Locate Key Facts (p. 60)

B. Practice

1. Monday–Friday, 8 A.M. to 5:00 P.M.
2. full-time
3. waitress, Jones' Family Restaurant, 12 N. State St., $5/hr.
4. Central High School, Middleton, attended 4 years, graduated
5. Mr. Prado, Ms. Frye, 555-7643, both teachers

▼ Lesson 6

After You Read (p. 69)

A. 1. False 5. False
2. True 6. False
3. False 7. True
4. True 8. True

Think About It: Identify the Main Idea (p. 70)

B. Practice

Sample answers:

Actively Search

Paragraph 2 Main Idea: Talk to friends, relatives, and job specialists about your job search.

Paragraph 3 Main Idea: Read want ads and look for signs and notices.

Paragraph 4 Main Idea: Job hunting takes a lot of work.

Knock on the Right Doors

Section Main Idea: Identify your network to find out who can help you.

Prepare for an Interview

Section Main Idea: Prepare for an interview by learning about the company, preparing questions to ask, and planning answers to questions you might be asked.

▼ Writing Skills Mini-Lesson: Fixing Run-on Sentences (p. 74)

There are different ways to fix the run-ons. Here are some examples:

Practice

1. The store needed a clerk. I filled out an application.
   The store needed a clerk, so I filled out an application.
2. The manager interviewed me. I was a little nervous.
   When the manager interviewed me, I was a little nervous.
3. I liked the manager. She seemed like a fair boss.
   I liked the manager because she seemed like a fair boss.
4. The interview ended. The manager introduced me to the staff.
   After the interview ended, the manager introduced me to the staff.
5. When I got home, the telephone rang.
   I got home, and the telephone rang.
6. The manager offered me the job. I wanted to think about it first.
   The manager offered me the job, but I wanted to think about it first.
7. It was a good opportunity. I decided to accept it.
   It was a good opportunity, so I decided to accept it.

▼ Unit 2 Review (p. 75)

Reading Review

1. (2) 3. (4)
2. (2) 4. (3)

Unit 3 A Sense of Community

▼ Lesson 7

After You Read (p. 82)

A. 1. True   5. True
    2. False   6. False
    3. True   7. False
    4. False   8. True

Think About It: Recognize Problems and Solutions (p. 83)

B. Practice

Sample answers:

Step 1: Teenagers need something to do.

Step 2: Community centers are geared to younger children. Teenagers need their own centers to go to.

Step 3: Build a sports-o-rama or a pool hall just for teens; adults pull together and do what needs to be done

Life Skill: Use a Phone Book (p. 86)

1. 555-5000
2. Senior Citizens Services
3. 911

▼ Lesson 8

After You Read (p. 91)

A. 1. a. False   e. True
      b. False   f. False
      c. True   g. True
      d. False   h. True
   2. number 2
   3. number 9
   4. number 10

Think About It: Follow Directions (p. 92)

B. Practice

1. The Tot Lot
2. The Parkman Bandstand

▼ Lesson 9

After You Read (p. 101)

A. 1. (3)   3. (3)
   2. (2)   4. (1)

Think About It: Locate Key Facts (p. 102)

B. Practice

1. **What?**   Community Folk Sing
   When?   July 10 at 7:00 P.M.
           Rain date July 12 at 7:00 P.M.
   Who?   Andy Wilkins
   Where?   Centerville Library Courtyard

2. **What?**   Library Network Computer Catalog
   Why?   to search for titles, subjects, or authors
   Where?   first floor, Room 100
   When?   during regular library hours (once a month is also a possible answer)

▼ Writing Skills Mini-Lesson: Correcting Usage Problems (p. 106)

There are different ways to correct some of the usage problems. Here are some examples:

The teenagers in my neighborhood didn't have anything to do, and they had nowhere to go. They made noise and littered, but the biggest problem was the fear they caused in the community. Some of the older people were afraid to go out. Finally, we held a community meeting and decided to start a sports program. Now the program is running well, and we don't have any more problems.

▼ Unit 3 Review (p. 107)

Reading Review

1. (2)   2. (2)   3. (4)

Unit 4 Crime and the Law

▼ Lesson 10

After You Read (p. 116)

A. Wording will vary.

1. Linda Brown was black, and the school was segregated, a "whites only" school.
2. He sued the Topeka Board of Education to end segregation.
3. Anyone accused of a crime has the right to legal representation.
4. (1) the right to remain silent

(2) the right to a court-appointed attorney

(3) the right to have an attorney present during questioning

5. (2)

Think About It: Apply Information (p. 117)
B. Practice

Anyone accused of a crime has the right to a court-appointed lawyer.

Life Skill: Read a Bar Graph (p. 119)
Practice

1. about 160,000 female lawyers in 1991. Your number may vary.
2. The numbers increased for both male and female lawyers.
3. There were fewer female lawyers in all years.

▼ Lesson 11

After You Read (p. 123)

A. 1. False   6. True
2. True   7. False
3. True   8. False
4. False   9. False
5. False   10. True

Think About It: Identify the Main Idea (p. 124)
B. Practice

1. My neighborhood has cleaned out the drug gangs.
2. We were all much safer 40 years ago.
3. Sample answer: I am not afraid of crime or criminals.

Life Skill: Analyze a Political Cartoon (p. 127)
Practice

1. Barely Moving
2. a heavy load of crime-related court cases
3. no
4. Sample answer: The U.S. justice system is so overloaded with cases that it can barely move, and may in fact topple over.

▼ Lesson 12

After You Read (p. 132)

A. 1. (2)   3. (2)
2. (4)   4. (1)

Think About It: Follow a Sequence of Events (p. 133)
B. Practice

Possible answers follow. You may have combined some of the events.

2. A man got out.
3. He went up to the Jiffy Mart.
4. The first robber put the shotgun back in his pants.
5. He got the bag of money situated under his arm.
6. He walked to the front of the store.
7. The other fellow got near the door, where the two robbers met.
8. The second robber pulled out his pistol.
9. He put his pistol into the first robber's face.
10. The second robber backed the first robber into the store.
11. The first robber dropped the bag of money.

Life Skill: Read a Parking Ticket (p. 137)
Practice

1. the fines will increase from $5.00 to $7.00
2. at least 10 feet away
3. no
4. the driver's license will not be renewed; the car owner's registration will not be renewed

▼ Writing Skills Mini-Lesson: Using Apostrophes Correctly (p. 138)

Last year, Katrina Smith's car was stolen. The police found it, but its hubcaps were missing. Now Katrina's car has an alarm. It's very loud, and it sometimes goes off when other people's cars get too close to it. Even children's bicycles can set it off. The neighbors don't like it at all. Katrina is concerned about her neighbors' complaints, but she's worried about her car, too.

▼ Unit 4 Review (p. 139)

Reading Review
1. 3, 1, 5, 2, 6, 4
2. (3)

Writing Skills

This handbook reviews the information you learned in the Writing Skills Mini-Lessons in this book.

Fixing Sentence Fragments

A **complete sentence** contains a complete thought. It must have a **subject** (who or what the sentence is about) and a **verb** (what the subject does or is). A **clause** is a group of words that has a subject and a verb. A clause can be **independent** or **dependent.** A sentence is an **independent clause,** because it stands alone. A **sentence fragment** does not contain a complete thought. It cannot stand alone. Here are three kinds of fragments and two ways to fix each one.

1. **Fragment:** Candy, donuts, and potato chips.

    This fragment has no verb. It does not make sense all by itself. To fix it, you must make the fragment into a complete sentence. Add a verb and any other words needed to make a complete thought:
    *   Candy, donuts, and potato chips **are bad for your health.**
    *   **You should avoid** candy, donuts, and potato chips.

2. **Fragment:** If you want to be healthy.

    This fragment is a dependent clause standing alone. Although it has a subject *(you)* and a verb *(want),* it is not a complete thought. It does not make sense all by itself. To fix it, you can add an independent clause to make the sentence complete. Add a comma after the dependent clause if it comes first.
    *   If you want to be healthy, **you must eat right.**
    *   **You must eat right** if you want to be healthy.

3. **Fragment:** Eating a lot of fruits and vegetables.

    This fragment also is not a complete thought. It does not make sense all by itself. To fix it, you can add an independent clause. You can also add a verb and any other words needed to make a complete thought:
    *   **They have been** eating a lot of fruits and vegetables.
    *   Eating a lot of fruits and vegetables **can help you stay healthy.**

Fixing Run-on Sentences

A **run-on sentence** has two or more independent clauses run together with no connecting word or punctuation. When you write complete, separate sentences, your ideas are easy to understand. If you run your sentences together without using connecting words, your ideas will not be clear. Run-on sentences are hard to read. Look at these examples:

- I want a new job I need to make more money.
- I have to start a job search it takes a lot of time.

Here are three ways to fix run-on sentences like the ones above.

1. **Divide the run-on into separate sentences.** Each sentence will have its own *subject* and *verb,* start with a *capital letter,* and end with a *period.*
   - **I want** a new job. **I need** to make more money.
   - **I have** to start a job search. **It takes** a lot of time.

2. **Use a comma and a connecting word like *and, but, or,* and *so* to join two complete sentences.**
   - I need to make more money, **so** I want a new job.
   - I need to start a job search, **but** it takes a lot of time.

3. **Use connecting words like *when, after, because,* and *although* to join a dependent clause and an independent clause.** Remember to add a comma if the dependent clause comes first.
   - I want a new job **because** I need to make more money.
   - **Because** I need to make more money, I want a new job.
   - I have to start a job search **although** it takes a lot of time.
   - **Although** it takes a lot of time, I have to start a job search.

Correcting Usage Problems

There are some problems that many people have when using written English. When you write, watch out for these common usage problems.

1. **Do not use a double negative.** Use only one negative word or word part (*no, not, n't, none*) to express a negative idea.
    Wrong: The teenagers did**n't** have **nothing** to do.
    Right: The teenagers did**n't** have **anything** to do.
    Right: The teenagers had **nothing** to do.

    Wrong: They could**n't** go **nowhere**.
    Right: They could**n't** go **anywhere**.
    Right: They could go **nowhere**.

2. **Do not use double comparisons.** Most one-syllable words are compared by adding the suffixes *-er* or *-est*. Longer words are usually compared using the words *more* and *most*. Do not use both forms together.
    Wrong: They were **more** tall**er**.
    Right: They were tall**er**.

    Wrong: They were **most** fast**est**.
    Right: They were fast**est**.

    Wrong: This game is the **most** important**est**.
    Right: This game is the **most** important.

3. **Use the word *good* to describe a person, place, or thing. Use the word *well* to describe an action.** *Good* tells what someone or something is like. *Well* tells how something is done.
    Wrong: They play **good**. They are **well** players.
    Right: They play **well**. They are **good** players.

    Wrong: That cake tastes **well**. She cooks **good**.
    Right: That cake tastes **good**. She cooks **well**.

Using Apostrophes Correctly

An **apostrophe** (') is a punctuation mark that is used two different ways:

1. To form a *contraction.* Put the apostrophe in place of the missing letters.

   It is the law ➡ It's the law.

   He does not know. ➡ He doesn't know.

   They will not try. ➡ They won't try.

   Do not steal. ➡ Don't steal.

   I am not going. ➡ I'm not going.

   She has not left. ➡ She hasn't left.

   We have not been there. ➡ We haven't been there.

   You could not have known. ➡ You couldn't have known.

2. To form a *possessive noun.*

   - **If the noun is singular,** add an apostrophe and the letter *s* (*'s*).

     The store of the man ➡ The man's store

     The rim of the glass ➡ The glass's rim

     The decision of the court ➡ The court's decision

   - **If the noun is plural,** add an apostrophe after the *s* ending (*s'*).

     The car of the robbers ➡ The robbers' car

     The house of our neighbors ➡ Our neighbors' house

   - **If the plural noun doesn't end in *s*,** add apostrophe *s*. (*'s*)

     The voice of the people ➡ The people's voice

     The concerns of the women ➡ The women's concerns

> **Tip**
>
> Do not add an apostrophe
> - to form possessive pronouns: *its, hers, yours, ours, theirs.*
> - to form a plural noun.
>   **Wrong:** The car lost it's license plate's.
>   **Right:** The car lost **its** license **plates.**
>   **Wrong:** Those book's are their's
>   **Right:** Those **books** are **theirs.**

Word Recognition Strategies

There are two main strategies for figuring out unfamiliar words when you are reading: using context clues and breaking long words into smaller parts. When you are reading, you can combine these strategies to improve your comprehension.

Using Context Clues

When you come to an unfamiliar word in your reading, the words and sentences around it can provide hints. These hints are called **context clues.** Context clues can help you recognize words and figure out the meaning of unfamiliar words. Here are some tips for using context clues to figure out word meanings.

Tips

1. Look for clues to the meaning *after* the unknown word. Look later in the same sentence or in later sentences in the paragraph.
2. Look for a definition of the unknown word in the same sentence or the next sentence.
3. Look for examples to help explain the unknown word.

Recognizing Long Words

If the unknown word is a long word, here are three word division strategies you can use, together with context clues, to help you recognize the word:

1. **Dividing Compound Words**

   A **compound word** is a word made up of two or more words. You can divide a **compound word** into its smaller words: *waste / basket*

   Tip

   If you are reading and come to a word that you don't recognize, see if it has smaller words in it that you do recognize. *waste / basket*

2. **Dividing Words with Prefixes, Roots, and Suffixes**

   Many longer words are made up of word parts called **prefixes, roots,** and **suffixes.** You can divide these words into those parts. The **root** is the part that gives the basic meaning to the word:

   port means "to carry"

A **prefix** is a part added to the beginning of the root to give it a different meaning:

trans means "across"
transport means "to carry across"

A **suffix** is a word part added to the end of a root. Suffixes can change the meaning of the word. They can also change how the word is used in a sentence:

-ation indicates an action or process
transportation means "the process of carrying something across an area"

Tip   When you don't recognize a word, look for a prefix, a root, and a suffix. Read the root first. Then add the prefix and the suffix. If you add the meanings of the prefix and the suffix to the meaning of the root, you can usually figure out what the word means.

3. **Dividing Words into Syllables**

A **syllable** is a word part that has only one vowel sound. You can divide words with two or more syllables into those smaller parts. Here are some tips.

Tips
1. Divide between vowels that have separate sounds: i de a   qui et
2. Do not divide between vowel pairs that make one sound.
   A. **Long vowel pairs:**   eas i er   mov ie
   B. **Other vowel pairs:**   poi son   coun cil
3. Do not divide vowel-consonant clusters: par ent   tow el
4. Divide between double consonants: dol lar   rub ber
5. Divide between a consonant and a blend or digraph: mer chant   en try
6. Divide before a consonant plus *le* at the end of a word: cou ple

Remember: There are exceptions to all these tips. If you say a word you don't recognize the first time you try, try another pronunciation. Keep trying until you hear a word you recognize. Then check it against the context of the reading to see that it makes sense.

The Writing Process

The Writing Process is a series of stages that can help you create a good piece of writing. These stages are shown below.

1. Prewrite, or plan your writing.
- **A.** Think about your topic.
- **B.** List ideas about your topic.
- **C.** Organize your ideas.
  - Decide which ideas you will use.
  - Decide how you will order them.

2. Write a first draft.
- **A.** Use your ideas from stage 1.
- **B.** Write about your topic.
  - Clearly state your main ideas.
  - Give appropriate facts, examples, or reasons to support your main idea.

3. Revise your first draft.
- **A.** Check that your draft
  - ____ includes your important ideas
  - ____ develops the topic with appropriate facts, examples, or reasons
  - ____ is clear and easy to understand
- **B.** Make changes to improve your writing.
  - You can add, cross out, or move information.
  - You can reword sentences

4. Edit your work.
- **A.** Check your draft for errors in
  - ____ complete sentences
  - ____ correct spelling
  - ____ correct punctuation
  - ____ correct capitalization
  - ____ correct usage
- **B.** Correct any mistakes you find. If you need help, use Writing Skills that begin on page 154 or ask your instructor.

5. Recopy your draft.
- **A.** Write a final draft. Include all of your revising and editing changes.
- **B.** Compare your first and final drafts. Note improvements.
- **C.** Share your final draft with a classmate, a friend, or your instructor.